The World Corona Changed

This concise book addresses the new geopolitical realm which will ensue from the coronavirus pandemic, exploring how the main international actors will position themselves in the post-Covid-19 realities. Contrary to some analysts, the author argues that, rather than an acceleration of existing or latent trends, the post-coronavirus world will present novel and otherwise unexpected features and challenges. Even the previously ongoing tension between the US and China will morph into an additionally complex and multidimensional puzzle, making it much more difficult to manage. In this book, the author provides a few basic tools for further analysis of the evolution of the new world situation, in an innovative way. Two main axes orient how analyses will be performed: the shape and evolution of the US–China relationship (and their interactions with other international actors), and the degree of co-operation – for example, on climate change and security arrangements – in the transformed world. The author suggests that the pandemic will be responsible for new emergences and fractures, and yet our ever more divided world will at the same time support unifying forces and links, highly dependent on technological developments being shared and/or protected.

The primary objective of this book is to draw a broad picture which will serve as a frame of reference for analysing how the community of international actors will react to major challenges – be they expected or unanticipated – in the post-pandemic world. It will be of immense interest to analysts, academics, politicians and students of international relations, geopolitics, strategy and world affairs.

Renato G. Flôres Jr. is Director of the International Intelligence Unit and Professor in the Graduate School of Economics at the Fundação Getulio Vargas (FGV), Rio de Janeiro, Brazil.

Innovations in International Affairs
Series Editor: Raffaele Marchetti, LUISS Guido Carli, Italy

Innovations in International Affairs aims to provide cutting-edge analyses of controversial trends in international affairs with the intent to innovate our understanding of global politics. Hosting mainstream as well as alternative stances, the series promotes both the re-assessment of traditional topics and the exploration of new aspects.

The series invites both engaged scholars and reflective practitioners, and is committed to bringing non-western voices into current debates.

Innovations in International Affairs is keen to consider new book proposals in the following key areas:

- **Innovative topics**: related to aspects that have remained marginal in scholarly and public debates
- **International crises**: related to the most urgent contemporary phenomena and how to interpret and tackle them
- **World perspectives**: related mostly to non-western points of view

Titles in this series include:

States, Civilisations and the Reset of World Order
Richard Higgott

Pivot Cities in the Rise and Fall of Civilizations
Ahmet Davutoğlu

Translated from the Turkish edition by Andrew Boord
Civilizations and World Order
Edited by Elena Chebankova and Piotr Dutkiewicz

For more information about this series, please visit: https://www.routledge.com/Innovations-in-International-Affairs/book-series/IIA

The World Corona Changed

US, China and Middle Powers in the New International Order

Renato G. Flôres Jr.

LONDON AND NEW YORK

First published 2022
by Routledge
2 Park Square, Milton Park, Abingdon, Oxon OX14 4RN

and by Routledge
605 Third Avenue, New York, NY 10158

Routledge is an imprint of the Taylor & Francis Group, an informa business

© 2022 Renato G. Flôres Jr.

The right of Renato G. Flôres Jr. to be identified as author of this work has been asserted by him in accordance with sections 77 and 78 of the Copyright, Designs and Patents Act 1988.

All rights reserved. No part of this book may be reprinted or reproduced or utilised in any form or by any electronic, mechanical, or other means, now known or hereafter invented, including photocopying and recording, or in any information storage or retrieval system, without permission in writing from the publishers.

Trademark notice: Product or corporate names may be trademarks or registered trademarks, and are used only for identification and explanation without intent to infringe.

British Library Cataloguing-in-Publication Data
A catalogue record for this book is available from the British Library

Library of Congress Cataloging-in-Publication Data
Names: Flores, Renato Galvão, author.
Title: The world corona changed : US, China and middle powers in the new international order / Renato G. Flôres Jr.
Description: Abingdon, Oxon ; New York, NY : Routledge, 2022. | Series: Innovations in international affairs | Includes bibliographical references and index.
Identifiers: LCCN 2021021883 (print) | LCCN 2021021884 (ebook) | ISBN 9780367763831 (hardback) | ISBN 9780367763855 (paperback) | ISBN 9781003166726 (ebook)
Subjects: LCSH: United States—Foreign relations—China. | China—Foreign relations—United States. | United States—Foreign relations—21st century. | China—Foreign relations—21st century. | Middle powers. | International cooperation. | World politics—21st century. | COVID-19 pandemic, 2020— —Political aspects.
Classification: LCC E183.8.C5 F56 2022 (print) | LCC E183.8.C5 (ebook) | DDC 327.73051—dc23
LC record available at https://lccn.loc.gov/2021021883
LC ebook record available at https://lccn.loc.gov/2021021884

ISBN: 978-0-367-76383-1 (hbk)
ISBN: 978-0-367-76385-5 (pbk)
ISBN: 978-1-003-16672-6 (ebk)

DOI: 10.4324/9781003166726

Typeset in Times New Roman
by codeMantra

Navegar é preciso, viver não é preciso.

(*Navigating is necessary, living is not necessary.*)

An old Roman saying, to encourage reluctant mariners, used as the central theme in a famous poem by Fernando Pessoa (1888–1935; Lisbon).

Contents

Preface ix
Acknowledgements xi

1 **Introduction: two guiding axes, multiple actors and shifting alliances** 1
   1.1 A matter of perceptions, choices and assumptions 1
   1.2 Two guiding axes 8

2 **The China-US relationship** 11
   2.1 Facts, fiction and scope of US-China affairs 11
   2.2 The likely evolution of the US-China relationship 14
      2.2.1 The pre-Covid-19 situation 14
      2.2.2 The probable future (mis)behaviour 18

3 **Reaction I: the fate of international institutions** 23
   3.1 The state of the Bretton Woods system; two examples 23
   3.2 Multilateralism at peril? Needed changes and how they could ideally take place 30
   3.3 The forgotten though existing institutions 34

4 **Reaction II: placing the other countries** 37
   4.1 Middle powers: a possible inventory 37
   4.2 Regional groups, associations and the fate of regionalism in general 48
      4.2.1 The European Union (EU) 50
      4.2.2 The Islamic world 52
   4.3 Shifting alliances, moving regional interactions 53

5	**A main issue and a major example: the digital complex**	59
	5.1 After the pandemic: the New Digital? 59	
	5.2 Dependencies, impacts and riddles 62	
	5.3 A plethora of other issues: which role in the reallocation of power and alliances? 67	
6	**Outlining scenarios: dynamic sketches, detailed analyses**	72
	6.1 Building blocks 72	
	6.2 Adding actors and problems 73	
	6.3 Building blocks redux 77	
	6.4 Selected scenarios 78	
7	**Conclusion**	87
	7.1 A not very optimistic reality 87	
	7.2 Is there another side? 89	
	Bibliography	91
	Index	93

Preface

The cov.vars.2 virus has been teaching several lessons to all of us. To begin with, besides the disarray it has provoked on the mathematical modelling of epidemics, with its multiple-peaked curves describing contagion and deaths, it has raised challenging statistical problems, aggravated by disturbing missing data and classificatory issues. The poor use of sampling techniques in several ways – assess the spread of contagion, testing and fast information gathering, among others – to advise public policies opens a question mark on how planning has been conducted.

In the pharmacological and medical realms, it raised disagreements, contentions and until now unsolved puzzles. The different approaches to treat the infected, the debate on the adequate pre-emptive or initial-stage medicines and the multiplicity of vaccines, perhaps too quickly tested and approved, offer a wide ground for future research and cold-minded reassessments.

The virus has changed, mutates, is one of the mantras used to explain unexpected behaviour and contradictory outcomes.

But it would be remembered as a great scientifically provocative nuisance if its damage had been circumscribed to the above fields. It overlapped: it invaded and pervaded nearly every social aspect of life, besides killing and impairing people, it hurt their mental health, their vision on their own lives, the meaning of their acts – be it for bluntly avoiding the infection or when balancing the odds in doing something desired that might increase the probability of contagion. The perception of risk will never be the same again in the world.

Fear became common currency, ignorance assumed disturbing proportions. Meanwhile, lockdowns, closures of activities, switches from the presential to the remote affected the economy, from the bakery next door to the queues in the main ports of the world.

A global phenomenon, a moment of reckoning for several beliefs, standard practices and supposedly solid knowledge. It gave full exposure to our laziness, ineptitude and tantalizing, false rhetoric on catastrophe managing and international co-operation.

At the time of writing these lines, the pandemic thrives on, and nobody knows whether it will enter a more controlled phase during the second semester of 2021 or it will linger on for one extra year.

It would be preposterous, if not starkly foolish to make predictions on the order that will eventually take shape. This *Gestalt* is now outside our possibilities.

The present short book has a much more modest objective. It intends to draw a few lines indicating how the global geopolitics may present itself soon after this much-expected moment, when the pandemic clearly diminishes for good.

It is prospective and it is short lived. The emerging order, dominated by the US-China relationship but conditioned by middle powers and other actors, like the international institutions, will be a transitory order.

During the pandemic, yesterday and tomorrow, elections took place, administrations changed and conflicts remained subdued or were heightened; the book tries to grasp this changing reality, the basic patterns of the coming (re-)arrangements.

A treasure chest of issues and problems is open to anyone who ventures into such a task. Selections must be made. As extensively announced and excused in the first chapter, my omissions inform about my viewpoints and final choices.

The great and unique Jorge Luis Borges continually reminded us that a book vanishes, once finished by its author. From that moment onwards, it will be recreated, silently rewritten in the minds of each future reader.

All who kindly spend some time reading this text will judge the version they have contrived, good, bad or incomplete: it does not matter. What I do sincerely wish is that every "new book" will act as an incentive for their reflections and thoughts on the world corona changed. An important exercise; a most needed duty.

Rio de Janeiro; Early autumn, 2021.

Acknowledgements

The labours involved in writing even a short book go far beyond the hours spent writing, reading, checking references and notes. They usually begin long before, in unending conversations, seminars, loose thoughts and questioning, less targeted reading and intensive observation.

For numerous years I have been concerned with objects and issues addressed in this book. To thank all the people who directly or indirectly helped me to forge my visions would be senseless. They were many, too many, including leaders, diplomats, civil servants and thinkers, present, implicitly or explicitly, in the text. I had the pleasure to make acquaintance and exchange views with them, during congresses or other opportunities, mostly in South America, Europe and Asia. They gave me their versions of recent historical events and shaped some of my impressions.

I thank the Editor of the series, Raffaele Marchetti, who invited me to expand my thoughts and perceptions on the sequel to the present crisis; a friendly and ever-encouraging colleague. I also thank those, friends and colleagues, who were open to help in the preliminary stages of the work: Adrian Pabst, Dan Hamilton, Mario Telò, Nuno Severiano Teixeira and Shashi Tharoor.

My institution, FGV, has provided opportunities that have contributed to my knowledge of several countries, people and problems. I believe fair to thank the institution in the person of its President, Carlos Ivan Simonsen Leal, who gave me room to strike a balance between the daily duties and the freedom to think without any constraint or partisanship. We have also entertained an active dialogue, and digressions, on many issues in the book.

The theme of the double has long fascinated writers and psychoanalysts. According to Edgar Allan Poe, William Wilson endured the bad luck of having a nasty and dangerous one. I am fortunate to have not

xii *Acknowledgements*

one but three: Dimitri Alexandrakis, Flavio Bruzzi Leite Guimarães and Heitor Pinto de Moura Filho. They have been instrumental in checking and questioning arguments and passages in the book, beyond performing a careful reading – punctilious in the case of Heitor – of preliminary versions. I state my debt.

My faraway brother Samir Saran has taught me much, through words and deeds, about India and its manifold nuances, and has always been a stimulating counterpoint to many views.

Rita Almeida Ribeiro has been indispensable for my personal welfare, and also a sharp critic and attentive commentator on key points in the book.

1 Introduction
Two guiding axes, multiple actors and shifting alliances

1.1 A matter of perceptions, choices and assumptions

The German philosopher, Georg Friedrich Wilhelm Hegel, said that every man or idea, philosophical ones included, is a product of its epoch. We are children of our times, and so it applies to the related historical events.

When, during the mid-years of the Ming Dynasty in China, by the third decade of the XV century, the Empire took an inner-looking attitude, concentrating for nearly a century on its internal development and consolidation; when, in 1787, a group of men, without any outstanding leader or genius among them – despite original minds like Benjamin Franklin's – decided to transform the 13 states originated from the former British colonies in the Northeastern side of the huge American continent into a version of democracy and federalism with strong future impacts in the world; when, in the aftermath of World War II (WWII), there was enough good-will among nations to accept a whole set of international institutions – some new, other remakes of previous ideas – that worked for about five decades; when, around the mid-1970s in the past century, a wave of authoritarian regimes started to fall, greatly due to economic failures; or finally when, in the post-1989 days, with the Berlin Wall becoming a rabble of stones to be sold as historical souvenirs, many people – some wrongly interpreting ideas of the very Hegel – saw the emergence for good of a unipolar world; in all these moments, the analyses, decisions, views and ensuing facts cannot be dissociated from the context of the epoch.

This book enjoys the same status, or shortcoming.

It is an appraisal of, or rather an essay on a short span of future years, starting in 2021, when the world will be living a (probably) last phase of a serious pandemic and rearranging itself for supposedly better times. It cannot avoid the heavy imprint of the recent events and

DOI: 10.4324/9781003166726-1

reactions, their related dialectic – to bow to another of Hegel's key contributions – and the whole context facing us.

In three to five years, many points here stated will have been either proven or disproven, but the value of the exercise goes beyond the number of its good shots. Building a framework of analysis for the coming times, even broad as in this case, obliges one to plunge deeper into the blurred day-picture, and identify, or rather choose the relevant actors, the key dynamics and the main axes able to condition outcomes. Reductions and simplifications are inevitable, and much ends up by being left aside. The gist of the exercise is to keep control of a small set of pieces – actors, structures, processes or ideas themselves – that allow to construct a feasible picture, or at least one that triggers, in other minds, useful thoughts and criticism.

To many, the coronavirus pandemic was a game-changer, to another large group, no: merely a catalyst for reactions that were either in progress or latent within the world system. A bit like the 2017–20 years of Donald Trump's foreign policy as President of the US, the virus forced behaviour or answers that were hidden or unexpressed, disturbed alliances, convictions and expectations – many having revealed themselves ungrounded or much weaker than imagined, led to their bare limit situations until then apparently solid and stable. In other words, it changed the norm, the normal and the normalcy.

It is not the purpose of this short text to discuss details regarding the way to classify the true role of the sars.cov.2 virus. Other difficulties, like the different perceptions on the narrative and analyses presented, are already significant. Indeed, as with the problem of the narrator in fiction literature, the facts of concern assume here a different meaning and relevance according to the adopted vantage point; the individual or layman's, the community, governments and organisations or a strategic thinker's one. The author stands in a falsely neutral position, trying to deliver a kind of omniscient and super-imposed message on trends, major points and highly likely developments: a to some extent futile and contradictory task.

But many things that occupy our minds in an international context are equally contradictory. The idea of multilateralism, discussed in Chapter 3 and popping up in other parts of the book, is full of contradictions and failed, maybe unachievable goals. The very "aggregation of preferences" – something already proved impossible by economists, implicit when speaking of a country like India, the US or Brazil, though anchored in the presumption that this is what the respective governments will do – is a well-known fallacy; useful and acceptable sometimes, disastrously misguiding in others.

If one admits the above, one should also kindly accept, or trust, that the author tried not to take sides, and avoided an aggressive, partisan rhetoric, particularly when tackling hot pairs and issues like the US × Russia relations, Muslim world and culture × Western, non-Muslim creeds and culture, Chinese views on territorial sovereignty × Hong Kong, Taiwan and the South China Sea, and quite a few others.

Turning back to Hegel, as acknowledged even by Bertrand Russell, in his caustic and critical, popular account of his philosophy in Russell (1945), he, along Parmenides and Spinoza, among others, had the important view that reality should always be taken as a whole. His "whole", however, was peculiar, perhaps innovative and certainly modern, as it was not to be conceived as a thing or a substance, but as a complex system, something resembling what was later called an organism. To concentrate on separate parts, disregarding this point, is to miss completely the right way to grasp reality.

Beyond the key actors in the context at stake, China and the US, other parts with a significant interaction with them have been incorporated in the debate, parts that could not be excluded from a minimalist, Hegelian "whole" that would give sense to the analyses. They resulted to be additional actors, middle powers and international institutions, and one concept, co-operation.

This essay thus claims that, armed with these elements, one can successfully draw schemes and scenarios helpful to understand significant global issues in the world corona changed, in the short to medium run. Holes and absences abound in the choices made, and the reader will be always – and perhaps rightly – able to say that, had country A or problem W been included, the analysis would have been sharper. The discussion of international organisations, in Chapter 3, does not address even one third of the existing ones, and deals extensively with principles and their justification or support.

The answer or excuse is that in the case of both countries and institutions, inclusion reflected the belief that those in are the ones which count most for the purposes of the essay. If a country, maybe an undeniable middle power, remained out, it means that, for the time frame at stake, and the level at which discussions and explanations are put forward, it does not count, or counts less; not that it is irrelevant, either per se or in a comprehensive world scenario.

Absence of a strict focus on certain themes and problems may also cause surprise.

There is no specific chapter on questions related to climate and the environment, though they enter arguments along the book. Both will surely regain relevance, supported not only by the myriads of photos

4   *Guiding axes, multiple actors, shifting alliances*

and graphs showing significant improvements in air quality in the major cities and the re-appearance of wild animals and birds in the fringes of several conurbations,[1] but also as a tool or excuse for economic revival and a different, positive global concern. The comeback of the US to the Paris Agreement will add more momentum to this, at least in media terms.

But will this debate, in a context of so many disputes and resistance to sensibly tackle global issues, with fractured political regimes and societies, higher social instability and scarcer funds, really prosper? The choice made here reflects a belief that, in the short to strictly medium run, not much progress will take place, despite the great fuss, hopes and even trust that, particularly after the presidential change in the US, the theme will return, top and foremost.

Nobody denies that things will happen but, besides the sweeping rhetoric that will pervade the media, speeches and promises, they will actually be second order in the face of the understandable revival of global public health questions, the mending of political and global governance fractures, the rescue of nearly destroyed economic sectors and the myriad of decisions and transformations – many either akin to the digital complex or left behind the door until now – in dire need of being addressed.

The "Green Economy" and "Sustainability" labels may be used as triggers for new infrastructure developments and manifold financial and tax schemes. Important as they are, it is doubtful whether, in the near future, they will play a role beyond that of incentives for certain actions, not all necessarily efficient in actually helping the dystopian world corona made. Holistic approaches, rightly embedding the environment in, or fusing it with health and labour, ultimately equity issues, may be theoretically appealing but demand a longer and careful reflection, perhaps not in wont in the coming times.

The fate of the 17 UN Sustainable Development Goals, launched in 2015 by the UN General Assembly and to be fulfilled by 2030, will be a good check of the validity of the former statements. An encompassing view of the main world problems, with one explicit Climate Action goal, and at least five others related to same theme, the Goals have shown mixed success in the last years, achievements remaining below expectations and even the reasonably possible. The post-Covid renewed interest in some of them may end up as something a little more than a fuss, drowned by other concerns and deep practical disagreements on concrete actions.

Another reason, of a pedestrian character, is size: a choice had to be made between an entire chapter dedicated to either the environmental complex or the digital galaxy.

Broadly classifying attitudes and behavioural patterns during the pandemic as elastic or inelastic, the latter, opposed to the former, referring to those that will remain after the crisis is over, if not totally but to a sizeable extent, the digital complex is one of the realms where more inelastic and transformative patterns may be found. Coupled with its strong social and technological links, it is a mandatory factor for both conditioning and understanding the near future. Notwithstanding, this is a standpoint that may leave some unhappy or partially distrustful of the analyses to follow.

A second absence, even more dramatic, relates to the vexed theme of inequalities and the fact, in principle taken for granted at a first evaluation, that more rather than less inequality is to be expected. Many statistics and preliminary estimates support this view. According to the UN, 240 to 490 million additional people, in 70 countries, will enter or return to multidimensional poverty, a status comprising lack of several basic needs; of these, the UN World Food Programme estimates that 130 million will suffer from continued hunger, while the Food and Agriculture Organisation (FAO) claims that starvation plagues more than 34 million people at this very moment. The World Bank (2020), in a somewhat different approach, estimates that 88 to 115 million people will be pushed to poverty, thanks to the pandemic.

As minorities are over-represented in the lower classes, universally more affected by the infection and the lockdowns, they endured huge losses in large, unequal countries as the US, Brazil and India. But the chain reaction of disasters seems unending: poor children suffered more with the closure of schools and, in some countries, resorting to digital teaching further excluded them, something to damage their future overall education, ensuing new disadvantages.

Dwelling deeper on this issue would require an enlargement of the economic discussion, which has also been reduced to a minimum, and may acquire strong nuances depending on the chosen region or country. The point is absolutely relevant and duly taken into account when the discussion concentrates on scenarios, and permeates other arguments, in different chapters. Nevertheless, in a way similar to the previous justifications, up to the medium run, it is hard to envisage major changes to the situation, broadly translated into higher tensions and greater likelihood of social conflicts. This unavoidable worsening of social conditions will affect most solutions, and negatively add to many scenarios' conclusions, as those highlighted in Chapter 6.

A related topic, the expected behaviour of the financial system and its linkage to the recession or recovery patterns, has also been eschewed. Besides its more technical character, it was neither responsible for nor

6 *Guiding axes, multiple actors, shifting alliances*

directly hit by the pandemic. Mounting fiscal deficits, many spurred by the rescue packages, elusive credibility of currencies and the way international capital is used and invested will naturally affect the state of the system and, depending on the instance, be crucial for solutions; their analysis would however lead the argument to other areas and supplementary considerations.

A discussion of specific security issues, notably the complex question of a likely increase in all sorts of weapons of mass destruction, in contrast to a reality where expenditures should be oriented to diminish the burden the pandemic placed on the poor and the economy in general, will neither be made. It deserves a more specific and detailed consideration, outside the scope of this monograph. Security is due to become twice as important, as countries playing pivotal games – like Russia, the two big and several middle powers as well – will recalibrate options and strategic behaviour. A "chase for new alliances" will take place: a determining point for perceiving the proper outline, even if somewhat blurred, of the new international order.

Like the hero in Edgar Allan Poe's *A Descent into the Maëlstrom*, the developments here presented try to enable the reader to abstain from looking at the appalling descent, amidst furious whirlwinds shaking the boat and, by gazing at the vortex as a single entity, with its inherent dynamics, to perceive that downwards currents, once reaching the bottom, re-emerged as upwards ones. If he could safely steer the boat downwards and then catch an upwards current, he could be saved.

The initial chapters in this book try to depict an approximate though useful image of post-coronavirus behaviour, in order to enable one to identify in such a vortex upwards currents leading to expected outcomes or describing possible features of the new normal; something explicitly touched upon in Chapters 6 and 7. It seems reasonable to accept that different upwards currents may be possible, even ones in which themes less emphasised here, briefly aired above, play more important roles. Not only them, others may be considered relevant, as new approaches to increasing and better distributing world welfare or the impacts on democracy, or rather democratic values and solidarity.

The issue of values, as (often emotionally) addressed nowadays, is, in particular, kept under control; there is no intention in the text to engage in discussions on constructs like "universal values", much in vogue in the fleeting and unfortunate unipolar moment of the last decade of the XX century. The urge for such construct, after several crude examples that its pursuit went too far, has sometimes transmuted into a minimalist pledge for rule of law and democratic values. This only apparently simple synthesis contains already hidden assumptions and delicate points.

Rule of which law? Muslim law is, culturally, historically and, from a societal viewpoint, as valid as French law, for instance. Are many of the Western groups pledging for respect to rule of law prepared to accept a convivial relationship with Muslim law and precepts? Questions like interference, drawing borderlines, management of mixed communities or countries then abound, just to give one example, not to mention the treacherous, moving sands of "flexible sovereignty". And, if what is at stake is merely stable rule of business law, can it be separated from the legal environment in general, or of the chosen polity?

Identical problems may be raised to "democratic values", as democracies differ in many substantial aspects – Indian democracy, with its specific party, states and institutional dynamics, is not the US democracy, for instance – and, at the very inside of so-called democratic enterprises like the EU, largely ruled by a combination of technical autocracy and supranational bureaucracy though, members disagree on their views of the concept and, still worse, on the amount of effective power to give to an already established but still partially emasculated Parliament.

Advocates of universal values and, more ambitiously, universal solutions, like "capitalism" or "free trade", usually forget that popular movements, the masses in general, constituencies and countries as well need to embrace a common pursuit, a roughly common vision of the future for moving in unison towards any major goal. Abstract ideas, attractive or logically undeniable as they might seem, need something else to mobilise changes; hungry, jobless and sick people do not care for them, but rather for food and minimally decent job and health conditions. Fear, as seen during the pandemic, may be a great engine of change, especially behavioural change; hate and the feeling of injustice also.

Avoiding this minefield, whose proper treatment is the subject for many other books, this essay takes as granted, or globally accepted, the 1948 UN Universal Declaration of Human Rights, whenever a lighthouse of values will be needed, most times implicitly, in the discussion.

This does not deny that ideas on values and rights, or more generally global ethics, are powerful and transformative. They lie, naturally and unavoidably, behind all possible scenarios, together with key passions or desires, fear or power also. This leads to a related question, regarding standpoints.

8   *Guiding axes, multiple actors, shifting alliances*

The text presents *a Western view of future events*. Despite agreeing with voices like Kishore Mahbubani's that Asia will progressively become the main world focal region, the following narrative is heavily based on Western information sources, debates, perceptions and experiences. An effort is made to try to incorporate an oriental dimension, but it is nothing more than an effort. In an extreme statement, it is as if another, dual essay, the mirror image of this one, written by an Eastern author, would be needed to convey a more balanced perspective of the world corona changed.

1.2 Two guiding axes

In order to provide a methodological framework for checking and analysing scenarios, two axes have been identified. They direct and help to ascertain the likely outcomes for a given issue.

The first is the shape and evolution of the US-China relationship: a major background element that will condition most versions of a new normal. Though to represent all possible outgrowths of this relationship in a straight line is a crude simplification of a multidimensional interaction that may take forms one cannot compare as better or worse, for the purposes of framing the exercises to be discussed, a preference order is assumed. The possible prospects of the relationship thus make for a horizontal line, moving rightwards to better, more constructive ones, and leftwards to increasing levels of poor dialogue, hostility and separation.

The second is the degree of co-operation in the transformed world. The coronavirus epidemic reminded two important sides of this concept: how essential it is for coping with almost any transborder crisis and how fractured and weak it has proven to be in present times. Optimists believe that, partially thanks to this worrying double display, responsible for unfair decisions and acts, people and nations will be much more inclined to collaboration during the post-coronavirus reality. A unique combination of opportunity and incentive for building a dreamlike "international community" has been created.

Unfortunately, there is no evident causal relation to support this, and a neutral view on possible developments is adopted here. Some issues may encounter a more favourable mood for joint endeavours, others may even be hindered by lack of co-operation. Fear, insecurity thanks to risks imprecisely evaluated, fierce competition for key resources, goods and markets may easily enhance short-sighted, egoistic behaviour.

Guiding axes, multiple actors, shifting alliances 9

A vertical axis, moving upwards toward more co-operation, and downwards to less, crosses the US-China's one, and defines four quadrants where different situations can be analysed.

The idea of framing policy space into four basic quadrants conditioning more detailed or elaborate examinations is far from new; it has been used in several planning and forecasting endeavours. Recently, in an exercise pursued before the pandemic by the *Deutsches Institut für Entwicklungspolitik* (DIE) on scenarios for 2040, they were creatively used[2]; one axis roughly coinciding with the co-operation one here and another one opposing the will to create international, perhaps multilateral institutions to an increased practice of ad hoc coalitions to solve specific global problems.

Chapter 6, however, leaves clear that the point in quadrant-space where the scenario will evolve makes just for the start of the analysis. The emergence of different sets of actors, notably middle powers and international organisations – though in the short run the latter will perhaps have limited clout, conditions the final result, also nuanced by the assumed level of the recovery. A pattern of shifting alliances may be expected, adding flexibility and reducing somewhat the generality of the analyses.

The real outcome, like in a Hegelian organism, cannot be dissociated from the role of other main issues. The digital can be at the root of one problem, may turn another into something more serious or disruptive or may signal the way to a relatively feasible solution. In such encompassing approach, more items may be added and the present text mainly stands as an example of some select answers, or forecasts, and of how to use the conceptual tool box it describes.

The structure of the book thus follows the above discussion.

Chapter 2 addresses the two superpowers, the US and China, and the multiplicity of their relationship and likely evolutions. Additional actors are discussed in Chapters 3 and 4, the former dealing with international organisations, the latter with middle power nations. Regarding organisations, great attention is given to their logic and conceptual basis, as changes, reforms or improvements are meaningless without a clear view of these preliminary ideas. Middle power nations include those considered more relevant for global pictures; some absences may look, at first sight, surprising. Chapter 5 digresses on a key technological feature whose role and widespread reach became more prominent and assertive with the pandemic: the digital complex.

Chapter 6 draws on the four previous ones and, using the two axes described, analyses in greater detail three out of many relevant issues.

It is supposed to illustrate the methodology proposed. This is finished, with supplementary comments, in a concluding Chapter 7.

The information, events and knowledge in general on the pandemic, used in the text, are those until the end of the first quarter of 2021.

Notes

1 Improvements and appearances thanks to a less polluted and peopled environment, with humans confined to their homes.
2 The exercise is the outcome of a conference jointly organised by DIE and the Konrad Adenauer Stiftung, at the end of 2019; Sven Grimm and Silke Weinlich were its main co-ordinators at DIE. More information can be found at the Institute's blog: //blogs.die-gdi.de/ under the heading "Multilateralism without future – or the future of multilateralism?".

2 The China-US relationship

2.1 Facts, fiction and scope of US-China affairs

Since Deng Xiaoping's reforms of the Chinese economy, launched in 1978, a shrewd observer, knowledgeable of the manifold ups and downs, turns and returns of Chinese history, could perhaps foresee that the country, for centuries a mighty if not the top world power, would gradually regain this status in the international scene.

Progress was neither easy nor smooth, the complex interplay of the extremely peculiar and many times secretive party politics with the societal and economic dynamics then unavoidably triggered was responsible for explosive moments, like the Tiananmen Square serious incident, while the vagaries of the mixed economic system that started to take shape produced its own problems and conflicts. Corruption, crises in a semi-capitalist style, rural-urban massive migration, the ticklish accommodation of a new-born and much handicapped financial system, all plagued the emergent trajectory of the former great empire towards economic supremacy and the metamorphosis of a largely poor society into another one, still in the making, where millions of people were taken out of sheer misery and an ever-growing middle class began to appear.

Trade was a major engine for the transformation, and a wise dual tariff policy greatly helped the creation of two economies, side by side: one targeted to the production of export goods, whose needed inputs were imported at low or zero tariffs; another for domestic consumption where often the same input or product would enter under a different tariff regime. The top industrialised neighbours, notably Japan and South Korea, gladly moved low-technology industries to the capitalist enclaves carefully designed in the vast territory, and strong linkages through multi-country production chains were created. This practice was followed by US and European industries, attracted by the

DOI: 10.4324/9781003166726-2

very cheap and disciplined labour force, expanding and densifying the import-export network.

Amazing figures have been published and analysed, several times and everywhere, to the surprise of all other countries. From 1978 to 2007, annual GDP per capita growth was an average of 8,12 per cent, 745 million people were rescued from absolute poverty in 30 years, goods exports and imports, relatively negligible in 1978, totalled 281 billion US$ in 1995 and surged to 4,6 trillion US$ in 2018. In 2010, China was the top exporter and the second economy in the world, by 2014 its GDP overtook that of the US, in purchasing power parity: positions solidly kept until now, while it is expected that, in about five to ten years, it will be the top economy in nominal GDP. Between 2011 and 2013, the country produced more cement than the US throughout the XX century. In 2021, eradication of extreme poverty is to be attained, entitling Chinese society to be broadly considered as a prosperous one.

How did the West perceive this huge, fast and surprising mutation? What images or models framed the pictures they made of the current realities, their past as well as future evolution? Questions like these have triggered long studies and debates, a preliminary observation being that viewpoints did differ and the range of evaluations has clearly been broad and sometimes conflicting. Despite variety and disagreements, two points may be said to have dominated most positions.

The first is that the spectacular growth was seen as a good thing. Trade and business flourished, economic gains were more than palpable – notwithstanding the unending debate on outsourcing and the related loss of jobs in the West – and it seemed that a unified, widespread and networked world production system would eventually glue together all nations in the planet.

The second is that all this was regarded as part of a trend that would bring, in a not-too-distant future, the formerly isolated nearly one fifth of the world population to the orbits of the governance galaxy originated in the post-WWII Bretton Woods system. Human rights could raise the eyebrows of certain segments and politicians; the elusive concept of "lack of democracy" could be invoked either when indeed proper or as a convenient bargaining argument, but no major obstacle or danger was effectively foreseen.

Until 2000, it can perhaps be stated, no menacing-China was discussed as a major worry for the world, particularly the established powers, apart from its disruptive effect in some economic sectors, often associated with debatable though not necessarily unusual trade practices. But even this was supposed to be duly tamed, with the emblematic accession of the country to the World Trade Organisation (WTO), in December 2001. Part by sheer and clear economic interest but also as a demonstration of the positive outlook embraced in the two above points, this event marks the triumph of a view of China as the new and prospectively welcome capitalist kid in the block.

During a period spanned by a little more than ten years, at the end of the XX century, the Berlin Wall had fallen, the US emerged as an apparently uncontested hegemon and the European project underwent significant expansion; all trajectories implying a common trend towards a full, encompassing Westernisation of the world, from business practices to ideological principles, all couched by ever present, digitally supported media and entertainment vehicles.

It is not the purpose here to precisely identify a turning point when the ascent of China began to be considered a concrete menace, when voices, which since the last decade of the past century "warned" about the existence of a Chinese project that did not fit into the standard Western canon and expectations, gained momentum and started to dominate the analyses and forecasts. Some take 2003 as the year when the inadequacy and indeed failures of the US policies as a world hegemon became crystal clear, and "the fear of China" gained an explicit dimension. Graham Allison's book on a modern interpretation of the Thucydides Trap, Allison (2017), is a recent evidence that opposition, competition and even fear had overtaken a previously more optimistic and much less confrontational narrative.

From one side, it is somehow startling how people could imagine that a bigger, more economically powerful and active China would not produce significant changes in the previously set chessboard, and – supported by its ancient, undeniably strong culture and expertise of world affairs – would not try to leave imprints and visions in all spheres of the governance galaxy. From the other, the change in outlook and the increasingly negative attitude to China's positioning cannot be solely analysed as the evolution of a relationship opposing China and the rest. The whole world changed, the accommodation of the major sequence of events after the composed Fall of Berlin Wall-Dissolution of the USSR had its own further developments, other regions were impacted and the US with its domestic and foreign problems also. The change in perceptions or risk assessments of the Chinese ascent cannot be dissociated from the deep alterations that, exactly since around 2000, started to occur at a faster pace. If the facts might have long ago given a clue to the shape of situations to come, the fiction, contrariwise, added emotional if not hysterical posturing. War games, unavoidable clashes in several geographic choke points – like the Taiwan

Strait or the South China Sea – and oversimplified, zero-sum forecasts of drastic and fast changes gained enormous scope: became credible and expected. The noise heightened to the level of the signal.

However, at the same time, interactions continued to increase, links and relations did not cease to multiply and the two giants proceeded in a path of comprehensive enmeshing.

2.2 The likely evolution of the US-China relationship

2.2.1 The pre-Covid-19 situation

Analysis of the situation in the past ten years, leading to the pre-Covid-19 moment, cannot leave aside the key US dynamics, from roughly the 2013–6 second Obama administration to the years of the Trump presidency, particularly the three first ones. During this period, reinforcing and many times confirming trends noticeable since the end of the first decade of the century, US foreign policy, after the disastrous interferences in Afghanistan and Iraq – started, respectively, in October 2001 and March 2003 under George W. Bush – and the ensuing serious aggravation of the Middle East puzzle, entered a period that could politely be called of mild disarray, while both China and Russia became more assertive in their international standings.

The mixed policies of the second Obama administration, with the pivoting – of exactly what? armies, priorities, strategic design, funds, aggressive attitudes? – to Asia, a conjugate reduction of the presence in Afghanistan and Iraq, the re-establishing of relations with Cuba, the landmark agreement – independently of whether one is for or against it – on nuclear weapons with Iran and a more subdued presence in Africa and South America, were suddenly confronted, since early 2017, by the personality of President Donald Trump, a man with his own ideas on all these and many other issues in international relations.

In China, Xi Jinping became President of the People's Republic of China (PRC) on 14 March 2013, for a standard five years period, and progressively showed his ambitions of becoming a long-lasting leader. These were officially confirmed on March 2018, when the term limits for the Presidency were abolished and he inaugurated a new, *endless* ruling era.

Since the beginning of Xi's first mandate, other realities were manifest. China had acquired technology leadership in a few sectors, modern telecommunications prominently but not only, with strong positions in renewable energies – notably wind and solar, power generation and distribution as well as in many digital subsectors, among others. In a May 2020 speech, President Xi Jinping addressed the "dual-circulation theory", highlighting the role of internal flows in the economy, *together* with the continued external exchange of goods and services. The goal of consolidating a fully operational, mature domestic market could not have been made clearer.

If in overall terms the US continues to be the encompassing technology leader and major innovation centre, competition with China, in ever more segments, became unavoidable: more than a growing nuisance, there are sectors where the US has already lost its pole position to China. In others, like supercomputers – with game-changing impacts in military applications – the speed of progress in the Chinese side may overtake, in a few years, the present US edge.

Though at first sight something absolutely normal in terms of world capitalist dynamics – a similar configuration having taken place between Japan and the US, during the 1980s, the microchip *trade contentieux* being a major example of it – it actually has deeper roots, linked to the progressive loss of competitiveness in many sectors, due to excessive concentration and loose, debatable regulations that supported the incumbents.

Within the evolution of the international or global value chains (GVCs) process, China had significantly upgraded its position in several chains, relocating lower value-added manufacturing to other destinations, notably Association of the Southeast Asian Nations (ASEAN) countries, like Indonesia, the Philippines, Thailand and Vietnam. This increasing presence in Asia was combined with the assertiveness of its sovereignty claims on Hong Kong and Taiwan, as well as on disputed reefs and small islands in the South China Sea and nearby waters. At the same time, the country steadily scaled up as a protagonist in international organisations and major multilateral and global issues, like climate change and sustainable development. As of early 2020, four out of the fifteen UN specialised agencies were headed by a Chinese, while the number-two posts in seven others were also with Chinese nationals. Activity continues, to secure positions in important Departments and Boards.

Backed by substantial funds, it spread influence and partnerships in Africa, Central and South America, East Asia and Eurasia; if some of these ventures, like many in Africa, had already a decades-long or even longer past, others were boosted by the encompassing Belt and Road Initiative (BRI), an ambitious, sustained push to establish a common infrastructure and trade network in the spirit of, though, much wider than the old Silk Road. Creation of the Asian Infrastructure Investment Bank (AIIB), which began operations in 2016 and eventually attracted several EU members, together with a smart move that placed the (BRICS') New Development Bank headquarters in Shanghai, beyond allowing China the possibility of enlarging its share in the near future, placed the country as a major official player in development and infrastructure finance.

It is in this asymmetric situation of a rising and pervasively expanding China in world affairs, alongside a, in certain aspects, declining US, that Donald Trump enters stage. Mr. Trump was absolutely coherent with his long-stated views on how the US ("America") had been consistently retreating from a position of international supremacy, while costly affording without any concrete rewards, especially financial and monetary, for the security, and ultimately peaceful life, of most of its so-called allies.[1] This included countries or arrangements so diverse as Japan, Saudi Arabia and the EU, the latter particularly as regards NATO's funding commitments.

Since early 2017, one can perceive the two countries playing, or rather slowly dancing a rondo in which the Trump administration started to encircle and get each time nearer to a PRC that swiftly followed the rhythm when collision was not in sight, and avoided several faux pas, by overtly stating its allegiance to the multilateral credo and institutions, like the UN and the WTO, and its shared concern with the global commons, as the climate issue.

Eventually, there was not much room for rounding and turning in the negotiating ballroom and, on 6 July 2018, the US Customs and Border Protection began collecting a 25 per cent tariff on 818 Chinese products, worth 34 billion US$. China retaliated by imposing the same tariff on 545 goods imported from the US, valued at an equivalent 34 billion US$.

Escalating retaliatory measures followed, together with a long succession of threats, positive gestures, negative or encouraging talks eventually leading to a moderately reliable truce on 15 January 2020, when a Phase One Deal was signed, including rollback of tariffs. Simultaneously, since mid-2019, more vocal warnings – and up to now gestures – on crossing allegedly red lines in Hong Kong, Taiwan, the several South China Sea chokepoints and, more recently, the Uighur question in Xinjiang were heard in the West.

As mentioned at the end of the previous subsection, there are the facts and the fiction and, at their origin, the hidden motives.

Under the excuse of a trade war, that may have been appealing to Mr. Trump's domestic constituencies and more than a handful of US international supporters, lies an unavoidable technology war between both powers. The Phase One agreement obliges China to "stop forced technology transfer", strengthen intellectual property protection, among issues addressing currency manipulation and nontariff barriers to US imports. Telecom and digital enterprises, notably the ever-present Huawei, were usual suspects during all the negotiations.

A worrying technological challenge had already been perceived during Obama times; the couple Trans-Pacific Partnership (TPP) and Transatlantic Trade and Investment Partnership (TTIP) having been a bold move towards raising a fence around China, leaving it in principle insulated from future high-technology developments and their common standards.

The ensuing and accompanying trade relations – and later the associated production dynamics – would evolve in a unified space comprising the main Western economies, together with key developed and developing partners in Asia. The gunpowder for the modern shots in this war are the standards, norms and regulations, ensuring free flow of information and manufacturing capabilities along the vast integrated area, anchored by the provision of multiple services made as homogenous and compatible as possible.

Within an ever-cooler Chinese stance, with respect to the Western one, thanks to a few fundamental incompatibilities between the US and the EU – related to what, in the latter, could be called basic societal choices – and to Mr. Trump's views and impatience with long negotiations, particularly with the EU, the TTIP floundered. The TPP, closed at the very end of the Obama II mandate, was not signed by the US, again largely due to Mr. Trump's standpoint.

This significant interruption in such an assertive soft power movement turned a bilateral clash more likely. To raise temperature – and again faithful to Mr. Trump's negotiating techniques – the portfolio of disagreements and potential conflicts was made explicit, and tensions moved one step up, fuelled by indirect or not so encouragement of other allies involved in them, from Hong Kong to Vietnam.

The pandemic, ironically, put a halt to this crescendo, with a switch to a concentrated effort by the US for keeping pressure on being the Chinese the real culprits of the generation and spread of the virus, their alleged misbehaviour at the beginning of the crisis acting as important evidence. This acquired different tones and intensities – from demands of financial compensation to blunt accusations of calculated, terrorist behaviour – and produced unexpected spill-overs, like the US administration's decision to quit the WHO, in June 2020, already reverted by the new team at the White House.

With the pandemic slowly unfolding a somewhat surprising pattern, seemingly entering under control, in what looked like a first wave, that then resurfaced with intensity in many areas by October 2020, the natural question is "How will things between the two countries resume after attention can again move to other international, global issues?".

2.2.2 The probable future (mis)behaviour

As stated in Chapter 1, a basic point of this book is that two major axes will condition the New Order that will start to gain shape. The most noticeable one, the likely evolution of the US-China relationship, taking into account the pre-Covid-19 situation, the domestic constraints faced by each and the other main forces re-emerging from this (final?) phase of the pandemic, may be sketched. Though a detailed answer on the probable behaviour of both actors in the coming international scene is senseless, given the degree of uncertainty regarding the possible outcomes, some lines can be drawn, even if they might rather be taken as hypotheses.

The first is that the overall attitude in each country, towards the other, is not due to change. In the case of the US, this means that – independently of the result of the presidential elections – the more confrontational stance towards China is not going to suffer an inflection. Mr. Trump's escalation may bear his specific characteristics, but it is perhaps one of his policies that received a larger support from the population and politicians in general, having been nearly bipartisan. China is a national US-problem, and there are basic claims and anxieties that must be addressed independently of the party in the White House.

Given that Mr. Biden has been elected, reversals and alterations in the foreign policy will of course take place, but it is here assumed that as regards China, for the basic context just outlined, they will be more in form than in substance. An increasingly confrontational stance, depending on the perceived support it will receive from expected allies, is possible. Nevertheless, in the short term, the new administration will be over-burdened by demanding domestic issues, notably the pandemic, and its own empowerment, with less time for substantial measures in the foreign side, besides recovering traditional alliances and postures.

Of course, and especially when dealing with the ticklish and sometimes elusive Chinese diplomacy, differences in treatment and form count, but in a broad analysis they can be left aside: the technology war (Tech War) will be pursued, the moderately aggressive use of the choke points will continue and tension will be present in the relations with China.

From the Chinese side, things, as usual, will be more nuanced. While finger-pointing towards the country – more or less annoying or frequent, depending on how the new presidency acts – will persist, China will answer with its pledge for world co-operation and multilateral solutions. A pledge in many ways sincere as, given that the financial system will be in reasonable though weaker shape, a conflictual situation or a generalised unilateral and aggressive stand in the new reality is entirely against Chinese interests. Most lines of business, of all kinds, *must ideally go on as usual*, for the sake of still much prized development, stability and internal peace.

A governance and social system in constant mutation, the PRC needs the previous qualities to tackle new internal issues and challenges, in the financial and booming entrepreneurial sectors. The recent events involving the Ant Ma group and its founder and mastermind, Mr. Jack Ma, are a good illustration of the emerging problems, demanding quick and effective equating.

Though conscious that the above goal is ultimately impossible, China will in principle mend fences and be nice, as often as needed and endured, in order to prevent a disruptive behaviour that might trigger another, and now deeper, external crisis, particularly if coming from or clearly backed by the US.

Despite the goodwill gestures, likely to be continued well after the epidemic is under control, and the difficult economic situation both countries will undergo – the US more than China, at least in the short run – a sour relationship is forecast. With more or less emphasis and speed, depending on Mr. Biden's stance, a retreat in the global US position towards China seems unavoidable, with a clear reprieve in certain lines of business. In the defence front, a supply chain review, to cover key military technologies – including semiconductors, high-capability batteries and rare earth elements, has already been ordered by the President, while China proceeds to invest both in the modernisation of the force and in its enabling capabilities, especially logistics, at the operational level.

Businesses may change address – a movement already explored, some leaving Chinese territory, though preferably remaining in Asia. As the Tech War hardens, several third countries will be put in a difficult position, and the discords prior to the pandemic, mentioned above, will resurface, adding disruption and attrition to the relationship. And this will come not without costs and difficulties for both sides.

The multiple threads nowadays binding US and Chinese ventures, interests and endeavours of all sorts, from high tech, materials science, urban planning and artificial intelligence to academia and art markets, will – as an invisible entity – react, suffer and many times struggle to attenuate or countervail cuts and disruptions; briefly, the broad movements outlined in the previous paragraph. How far they will be able to sustain a more than operational relationship is an interesting point to watch.

No violent conflict or military confrontation – but for unlikely minor, low-intensity episodes – is forecasted though. The idea of a replacement of hegemons through violence – bringing back to the fore the Thucydides Trap, as argued in the already mentioned Allison (2017) – or of a blunt war is ruled out. Nevertheless, this demands a better qualification.

Neighbourhood relations are due to become more sensible and involved; in a less constructive relationship, China will be less tolerant with the US active presence in ASEAN countries and the nearby Korean and Japanese territories, with massive concentration of troops and the headquarters of the US Seventh Fleet in Yokosuka (Japan). The same applies, from the US side, to the increasing Chinese presence in Central America, Africa and Asia, and its continuous and slowly effective one in South America.

The whole situation is starkly novel, and bears no relationship with apparently similar periods, notably the Cold War, a comparison sometimes wrongly raised.

Interpenetration and mutual dependence are the name of the game, and each player will be forced to sleep with the (supposed) enemy, while striving to conduct its own policy. Both will have a nuanced but also fairly blurred view of their objectives, given the myriad issues and interactions at stake – and the related middle powers that matter in each of them, whose reliability cannot be taken for granted, being not at all clear up to which point they will want to pursue each and every specific difference or disagreement.

Notwithstanding, segments of the US elite may consider a drastic, hostile outcome as the ultimate way to assure the country's leadership. As prospects become ever more uncertain regarding the Tech War, resorting to the still superior military strength may be a way to keep supremacy. Excuses abound and can be easily magnified by cleverly directing public sentiment. In this vein, it is telling that a recent vision of a coming war, disguised as a best-seller novel, though co-authored by a well-known representative of the military establishment, Ackerman and Stavridis (2021), has been receiving wide coverage. To move from the book to a block-buster war movie would be a further signal that, for some powerful groups, resolution of the US-China relationship will be in the battlefield.

In a lower key, despite the impossibility to avoid deep if unwanted interrelationship, convergence is an idea, or ideal, of the past.

Separation, or at least, to use a buzz word during the pandemic, increasing *social distance* must be expected; how diplomacy will tackle this remains unknown. The distance will be less due to ideological divergences and much more to the objective of thriving and prospering without the other's presence and intervention, a desire stronger in the US than in China. As the declining power, recognition that, for instance, not absolute but greater leeway should be given to China in the South China Sea, as at the turn of the XIX century the US demanded from European powers in the Caribbean, is a painful, still far-fetched acceptance.

In this context, it is important to understand how priorities will be set in each nation.

If both opt for a too narrow view, or both leaders engage in a competition about who will set the tune in global issues like the environmental dilemma, or the reform of world trade, the gap will become larger and worrisome; if at least one of them, even out of self-interest, practises a reasonably broad view of its foreign interests – and China, at this moment, is the one more likely to adopt this – it will be a little easier to manage the ever more difficult relationship.

A point usually disregarded, if not fully denied, is that while the US clearly wants to keep a superpower status, China may prefer to have a considerable roaming space, proportional to its dimension and needs, but not necessarily envisages to lead the world in the fashion the US did after WWII, and still thinks it should. In a prophetic statement, 45 years ago, Sir Michael Howard already warned about the "outrages that have been committed against China by the maritime powers during the past hundred years", something unlikely to be forgiven by the country, Howard (1976). Redress, atonement and ultimately peaceful recognition may play a larger role than usually considered when analysing Chinese behaviour.

Global issues act as a double-edged knife, enabling joint and apparently friendly pursuits sometimes, but also eliciting the establishment of different factions and opinion groups, heightening separation. The amount of goodwill to co-operate in each specific issue, and the way middle powers will position themselves may change the nature of impasses and oppositions, hopefully though not necessarily in the direction of avoiding conflict.

It seems evident that "hunting for alliances" will occupy centre stage. The irony is that both are ill-positioned for substantial and enduring rewards.

The US will strive for a broad portfolio of allies ready to side with its global vision and the related possibly tougher consequences, as regards China. Its allies would prefer a quieter though solid US, and share mixed feelings towards its aggressive postures on extraterritorial and unilateral enforcement of its laws and economic sanctions, the pressing of unwanted policies and strategies and the debatable joint use of its global financial clout and the democratic values and human rights rhetoric. The latter, sometimes, in a clearly political and hypocritical fashion. As for China, the alluring power of no-strings-attached money may secure momentary or problem-specific support, but is no guarantee of a steady marriage. Moreover, each will cull and judge allies ultimately by the degree they will side with their strategy towards the opponent; a well-known way to forge unstable alliances.

The overall result is that within a difficult, sour and tense context, intensity – as opposed to moderation – will be the key variable; a variable whose control lies in the hands of each player. It is through this channel that the domestic component enters stage. Intensity is unavoidably correlated to the degree of internal support to the foreign actions adopted; a statement valid both in China and in the US, despite the different political regimes. In the world corona changed, it is hard to conceive the people in the two powers endorsing disruptive or war-prone attitudes. And both powers need a minimum of domestic harmony to muddle through the post-crisis environment and resume sustained growth.

The unpleasant aspects of the relationship, and their corresponding evolutions, may thus keep on going either as a background noise, or a persistent nuisance, or a sometimes close to unbearable but manageable conflict notwithstanding. Many communication channels are due to remain open and dialogue, under specific circumstances, possible.

But the devil never sleeps, tell most sacred books, and the harsh side may spread until interfering in many or even nearly all aspects of the labyrinthine pattern of interactions. In this event, more division and fragmentation will take place, forcing the secondary actors to also move to more rigid choices, certainly outside the interest of the majority of them. A world with a mild multipolarity may emerge, as some middle powers will counteract and, by gathering minimally credible alliances, try to keep a roughly identical distance from the two giants.

It is under these different levels of a basically worse relationship that the other elements of the setting must be analysed.

Note

1 Without debating his views, they were clearly stated, for instance, in Donald Trump's 1987 CNN interview at Larry King Live, among other similar pieces.

3 Reaction I
The fate of international institutions

3.1 The state of the Bretton Woods system; two examples

The discussion in the previous chapter naturally leads to expanding the set of actors, be they countries or international institutions. For the latter, the first important question refers to the future (or fate) of the Bretton Woods institutions – and that of further or supplementary proposals. This section addresses such question, with the help of two concrete examples, the World Health Organisation (WHO) and the World Trade Organisation (WTO).

Much has been written about the Bretton Woods order, its successes, shortcomings, failures and prospects. Its pre-pandemic state already demanded attention, if not urgent help. The combination of transformational world events with significant changes in the perceptions of main leaders and constituencies, as regards the objective and utility of many institutions, had already led to a reasonable state of flux in the system. Mounting global mistrust as to its need and efficacy was a reality.

Despite hopes that the Covid-19 crisis would be a wake-up call for reshuffling and strengthening the arrangements, multilateral institutions continue in a state of corrosion by multiple agents, conflicting objectives and unsolved issues. Ironically, the new, less co-operative world and its developments configure a moment when they are and will be most needed. Joint actions are nearly an essential condition for coping or, at least, alleviating the borderless problems that, with greater intensity and multiplicity, will plague humanity as a whole. Advocates of the proliferation of international organisations are already pledging for a "Global Risks Organisation", or similar constructs, for dealing with the new, coming planetary difficulties.

Prior to looking for novel creations, always costly in all aspects, it is advisable to see whether existing structures, if well transformed or adapted, may be able to cope with the changed reality, though great antagonism and fierce debate are likely to take place between partisans of each approach. Another alternative is to admit that the whole disposition became obsolete, or rather is in the process of metamorphosing into a new structure, whose basic features must then be identified.

Three broad propositions must be left clear, before engaging in any debate or forecasting exercise.

International institutions cannot be more than their members want them to be: they are a focal point to energies and efforts, a catalyst for effective common endeavours, a locus for the peaceful and constructive resolution of disputes and for addressing borderless questions, many related to the global commons. If discredit, suspicions and pre-empting oppositions start to plague the set of members, any organisation is doomed to become paralysed or considerably lose clout and efficiency. This means that before thinking of the constructions themselves, it is wise to check the surrounding, overall mood and prospects, given the prevailing power fragmentation, the internal problems in most democracies – resulting in high polarisation in some of them – and the not very encouraging signs of co-operation highlighted in the previous chapters. Does a minimal agreement that an existing or intended international institution will provide the required answers apply?

On the other hand, there do exist problems that require a multinational, preferably institutional approach. The pandemic left much clear how important a swift, flexible and highly operational international public health organism would be, as well as how, despite several shortcomings, the WHO played quite a few key roles during the crisis. The health issue, with its manifold facets, from prevention to vaccines, including the crucial information gathering and analysis task, will demand more and better approaches in the near future. But the way to institutionalised answers does not have a single solution; regional schemes can be envisaged, more modest thematic groupings may be created, formats with less bureaucracy though greater focus may be attractive and there will always be a powerful nation that might prefer to play it solo, despite how costly and difficult it may result.

This debate is not new: its opposing forces being well-known. During Bretton Woods' times they had also been at stake, but the post-World War II (WWII) mood opted, without much disagreement or discomfort, for a unified solution, centring around the UN separate structures to tackle specific major issues, from agriculture to air transport, health of course figuring prominently; an idea cherished by the late US President Franklin D. Roosevelt.

Is the world corona changed in a similar moment, with indeed a constructive revival being likely, or is there no more scope in it for the spirit until now prevailing?

Thirdly, relevant actors continue to multiply, posing the question of who should be included in a global arrangement. Beyond states, international NGOs – with their own agendas and internal divisions, transnational corporations with considerable impetus and more fluid entities, such as mass movements and minorities, or debatably independent units as specific markets and networks – may want to or be indeed relevant to have a say.

Beneath these three points, the question of metamorphosis, briefly addressed above and cogently raised by Beck (2016) in pre-Covid times, lies in latency. Is the effort to save, change or rebuild the present institutions not a waste time? In the aftermath of the crisis, should not most energies be dedicated to social-economic recovery and the establishment of multiple co-operative bonds, while the world waits a further while to let the metamorphosis in progress engender the different butterflies that might emerge? As Beck points out, doing nothing is doing something ...

Two examples may be enlightening; they show, in different contexts, how much progress – if the word makes sense – may be expected.

The WHO and the WTO

The first organisation deals par excellence with the health question. Though it is nowadays mostly under attack from several countries and experts, given its high exposure and sheer importance during the pandemic, the existing health order comprises other initiatives.

Examples are the Global Alliance for Vaccines and Immunisation (GAVI), now re-entering stage thanks to the whole debate, complex logistic operations and huge economic interests regarding the Covid-19 vaccines on the table, and one of the co-ordinating entities of the recently created COVAX, an alliance of 90 per cent of the world governments for globally providing their safe and effective distribution; the Global Security Health Agenda; the Coalition for Epidemic Preparedness Innovations; and regional institutions, like the Africa Centres for Disease Control and Prevention and the Pan-American Health Organisation (PAHO).

Beyond these less-known members, WHO's related International Health Regulations (IHR) are a major body of the international public health system.

The IHR, under the responsibility of the World Health Assembly, WHO's governing body, are a set of core legal prescriptions governing members' conduct with respect to infectious diseases. It is thanks to them that the Director General of the Organisation is entitled to declare the existence of a public health emergency of international concern, and request responses and adequate measures from member states.

In view of the above, and the more than minimally decent historical record of the WHO until now, it seems valid to argue that instead of cutting national contributions to it, and looking for other, perhaps regional solutions, the opportunity provided by Covid-19 to make a thorough screening and (re)shaping-up of the organisation should be seized. A task to be accomplished taking due care to maintain its substantial portfolio of key projects, maybe giving it additional powers and, mostly needed, more rather than less funds.

The funding issue deserves attention, as around 70 per cent of the budget is made of contributions – mostly by private foundations and entities – already ear-marked to specific projects of the donors' interest; around 20 per cent only is made of the official countries' shares (assessed, not ear-marked voluntary contributions). Without arguing how welcome any contribution is – a matter to be discussed elsewhere, the Organisation must have full control of its funds and, in principle, avoid being a channel for the performance of private, even if humanitarian purposes: a practice that opens a door to questionable goals.

Moreover, the Organisation, which jointly with the Coalition for Epidemic Preparedness Innovations co-ordinates COVAX with GAVI, should be entitled a tighter grip within the galaxy of institutions just described.

During the pandemic, governments have usually resorted to individual policies, avoiding or forgetting consultations, moderate collaboration or joint planning. Inside the EU, even for the decisions regarding control of the common Schengen border, harmonised policies were infrequent.

Vaccine production was largely the outcome of direct negotiations among country governments and big pharma representatives, disregarding global and equitable solutions; property rights have been tightly and egoistically guarded, forgetting that huge numbers of human lives were and are at stake.

In the EU, there was agreement they should be subject to a common purchase, though much ended also acquired on a country basis, bypassing either commitments or wishful statements and promises. The overall outlook was and still is of a lack of coherence and basic co-ordination of health and risk-management measures within the Union; something also displayed, in a broader geographical scope, around the Western hemisphere. The WHO, though not being either able or supposed to solve all the issues at stake, was consistently eschewed, whenever possible.

The case of vaccines is emblematic and deserves additional considerations. Competition in stark capitalist mode was the rule, with big laboratories rushing to be the first one to reap the huge funds allotted to the vaccination effort – from research, development and actual sales – and accrue the ensuing side benefits, notably in the financial and stock markets. Though from one side this has a positive effect, spurring innovation – many times, it must be said, funded by public money – and implementation, ultimately and hopefully saving lives, the near absence of international collaboration and better global allocation of efforts and resources has been blatant.

The race to approval and to fix advanced sales that later were not always honoured, the leonine sales contracts imposed on weaker governments, the sluggish multiplication of production centres in different countries, crucial to ease logistics and increase access, show that live animal spirits largely prevailed. The ruling principles of global organisations and pursuits, where to jointly struggle for the common public good is foremost, were quickly and pervasively disregarded. Could the WHO have played a better role, more assertive and sympathetic-to-all-world-regions in these dynamics, when wiser planning and fairer decisions easily vanished in the face of selfish, mainly economic motives?

For many countries, relationship with the WHO remained dubious and highly dependent on the particular moment or specific need. Travel bans, border closures and quarantine requirements for incoming persons, though authorised by the IHR to be autonomously imposed, provided they would be reported to the WHO within 48 hours of the imposition, were rarely informed. Complaints have been numerous, supportive gestures and measures scarce.

Will all these well noticed and registered attitudes, once times look a little better, set the grounds for an ideal and concerted move to re-empower the WHO along lines as previously outlined? It is doubtful.

The WTO was already under intensive care before the epidemic. Broad reforms seem a priority: the organisation went out of tune with the new trade realities and, without focus, aimed at partial corrections, missing the larger picture. To think that topical remedies like changes in the Dispute Settlement Understanding would provide enough oxygen to its breathless body is illusory.

28 Reaction I: fate of international institutions

After too many years in the hands of bureaucrats and international civil servants – competent as they might have been – novel ideas and ways to cope with the new "shapes and forms" in traditional trade in goods and services must be put to a full discussion, without prejudice or a hidden desire – as in Tomasi di Lampedusa's masterpiece, *Il Gattopardo* – to implement change in order to ensure that things remain as they are.

Jobs and ways for job creation gained prominence among the growing set of discontents with globalisation. Free trade, together with its booming global value chains phenomenon, may be a pathway to increased economic efficiency and profits to those directly, and sometimes even indirectly, involved in the game – neither necessarily nor always nation states, but other objectives, like securing employment to the less qualified, became imperative.

Moreover, the criticism originally raised by the US applies: the Appellate Body slowly became a dual persona of the institution, setting decisions and procedures that, gradually and informally, though effectively, became codified as interpretations of, additions or extensions to the established, hard negotiated treaties, and thus introducing an unacceptable amount of juridicisation to the Organisation.

While a well-intentioned Dr. Jeckill cared for an enlightened obedience to the treaties and rules, and a transparent discussion of their improvements, a young Mr. Hyde, now with a law degree, simultaneously created a world of sentences and views by clever judges, often hardly savvy trade experts, that moved in other directions, when not contrariwise, indeed creating a parallel world. Where to would this trend lead?

Notwithstanding, the WTO, like the WHO, has nowadays a precious cumulative value – knowledge of treaties, rules, schemes and procedures, embodied in its high-level staff – that should be preserved, and global trade in principle needs global rules.

Accounting for all sides of the puzzle is feasible though challenging.

Besides the Appellate Body conundrum, hot points are found in the new digital complex and its multiple trade-related aspects – a serious void at present in the Organisation; updating and rethinking of intellectual property rights, to be made more flexible in ticklish sectors like pharma – as shown during the pandemic, or more modern in brand-new ones as the digital galaxy, are needed. Points to be addressed under a new vision as regards trade and investment, where the balance between the micro-economic objectives and the broad social benefits will be even harder to achieve than in the Uruguay Round times. The same applies to the irksome question of state trading firms, which needs to begin with a clear, widely accepted definition of this animal.

The digital involves other actors, notably the big transnationals that operate comprehensive platforms, and will also pose difficult queries about representativeness. Not to mention the purpose of certain countries and blocs to impose extra tariffs on the grounds of how green the purchased good or service is considered to be.

Demands and disputes, independently of how dysfunctional the Organisation might be, will surge as trade patterns resume and evolve in the coming – two, three, more? – recession years; resort to domestic subsidies will frequently appear in multiple guises, the same with protectionist measures that will add to the significant set still remaining from the 2008 to 2009 financial crisis.

A temptation to separately deal with issues such as the ones above, under a pragmatic spirit of mending pressing misdeeds, repairing damages and taking the WTO out of intensive care, will be strong.

But is this sustainable, or the right course of action? And who will lead it, a US wanting to be again conspicuously present at every great ball it considers itself the chief dancer? Will China be happy with this choice, or will it in its turn try to control the orchestra? What about the likely coalitions? Given the multiplicity of themes and damages to tackle, it is hard to expect middle powers to stick to the same leader in all of them. Or, quite on the contrary, will a divide take place, with groups of faithful followers closing ranks behind either China or the US?

Again, must really something be done quickly, while underground, correlated changes take their due times to become reality? The right timing and comprehensiveness of the needed endeavour are disturbing unknowns at this moment.

Perhaps one great contribution of the pandemic is to turn the start of the post-corona world into an opportunity to rethink what do the big and middle powers want of a WTO? up to where should its attributions go? which sectors and rules should receive immediate attention, which constituencies it should incorporate and which other goals should perhaps nuance and make more human and contemporaneous the absolute free trade dogma?

This may stand as a neutral way to begin, likely to engage the greatest possible number of partners. International institutions are foundational for guaranteeing the rule of law in a global society that wants to minimise its inherently anarchic trends, but for this, a sizable number of countries must be willing, fighting for and supporting them: the WTO needs a rebirth out of a credible common effort.

Unfortunately, what may seem the right, safe starting point, maybe is not yet. At the heart of the previous statements lies a fundamental, preliminary option that the debate on both the WTO and the WHO clearly unveils: do nations in this new world order still believe in and want multilateralism?

3.2 Multilateralism at peril? Needed changes and how they could ideally take place

The great danger in the post-corona reality is that, as raised in the WHO and WTO examples, debates on reforms or options will take place – with each side having powerful supporters – while the institutions themselves will be dearly needed. How to reconcile future demands and changes with those of the present hard times may become a further stumbling block, prompting more impasse, paralysis and the search for second- or third-best solutions. A situation that may eventually lead the institution to a complete neglect, for failing to accomplish its fundamental tasks.

Less complicated challenges will perhaps be met by the International Monetary Fund (IMF) and the many development banks and international financial institutions, though pressures on them will also heighten. A litmus test for the latter, and also a crucial trial for the basic axes proposed in previous chapters, will be their capacity to co-ordinate syndicate efforts and funds for alleviating countries heavily hit by the combined epidemic-recession effect. In each of their members, domestic macro-economic problems and the queries of its own nationals – with some groups and segments heavily hit by the strict lockdown policies and their aftermath – will make for good excuses to scale down or abort more generous and effective programmes.

The pre-Covid state of flux will likely deepen in the short run, creating additional confusion to the world order and indirectly channelling power from the institutions to the US and China. Regional and more independent arrangements, like BRICS or the Shanghai Co-operation Agreement, may also gain more visibility but they themselves will need adaptations.

Some will claim for reinforcing and more decisively supporting the G20,[1] though its past record, particularly in recent times, raises doubts about its objectivity and effectiveness. Even so, pledges for a closer association between the G20 and the G7, and the creation of focus groups within them, to study and discuss the most pressing issues, will be heard. But how really representative would this be?

In the backbone of such *confusión de confusiones* the fundamental question at the end of the previous section remains: how desirable and effective the multilateral approach became, and how far, or for how long can it be determinant to all solutions envisaged?

In a state of growing anarchy, following Ikenberry (2020)'s insight, it is easy to think that big and main middle powers would be fully occupied by the "problems of anarchy", namely, hegemonic struggles, power transitions, competition for security, spheres of influence and reactionary nationalism. However, he rightly asserts, they are much more threatened by "emergent, interconnected, cascading transnational dangers", like pandemic diseases, financial crises, dangerously encompassing pollution threats and nuclear proliferation, to mention a few. International organisations fit in exactly here, as they are the preliminary step to tackle these real catastrophes.

This implies that there is neither reason nor evidence that in the new international order there will not be a context for such institutions. But why then, as in parts of this chapter, a pessimistic view has been put forward? The first global reason, hinted at before, is the discredit into which the Bretton Woods institutions have fallen, in a world and context different from those in which they were designed. No wonder some of them, like the WTO, a brawny successor of the General Agreement on Tariffs and Trade (GATT), are in dire need of care. The other reason is the key issue above: is multilateralism still as important as in the post-WWII moment? should it be the guiding approach to both the reformed existing institutions and the new ones that might be created?

It is then time to present a formal though restricted, operational definition of multilateralism for the purposes of this text. It means the institutional design which, to the broadest possible reunion of members related to the issues at stake, guarantees equal rights and obligations to all. In particular, all ideally share, in any matter concerned, the same amount of decision power, in the sense that to each is associated one equal vote. Members, in the present discussion, are usually states and, to a certain extent, multilateralism translates to communities of states the ideal format of democracy. Despite engaging, and having the desirable quality of equalising the weak to the powerful, it suffers from innate deficiencies.

While in the case of democratic nations, the monopoly of law enforcement and, if needed, violence is clearly in the hands of the state, as Max Weber analysed at the turn of the XIX century, in an international multilateral organisation no police force is available. The means to ensure the due settlement of disputes assume different forms, none ideal or fully efficient. Moreover, the imposed *a priori* equality may generate distortions particularly as regards obligations. In GATT and WTO rules, to assume all members equally wealthy, developed and competitive is, sometimes, a cynical way to push them towards the model and interests of the powerful; in the case at stake, the advanced Western economies.

Bigger, more powerful countries can always put pressure on smaller and weaker ones to accept their views, many times through bargaining their support against concessions in other areas, like a foreign debt or a desired military aid. This kind of "corridor politics or bartering" is inherent to multilateral organisations, from the UN to the WTO, where they are sometimes called "Green Room meetings". Corridor politics do not invalidate the merits of multilateralism, but introducing mechanisms to curb them is a welcome though not easy advancement, as they should not impair one of the golden tools of multilateralism which is the coalition of the weaker at a level and size able to block the strong.

At the same time, muscular members can break the rules and refuse to join arrangements nevertheless supported by them. The refusal of the US to be a signatory of the UN Convention on the Law of the Seas and, more crucial, of the International Criminal Court, then followed by China, Russia and, under the US shield, Israel, shows the limits of acceptance of this supposedly ideal design.

On the other hand, the powerful sometimes play the magnanimous, closing their eyes to the strict obeyance of rules by others, in the aim of garnering new friends or adepts. Trade provides once again a good example. The acceptance of India at the GATT, out of Cold War strategies, in 1948, with around one third of its tariffs uncapped, raises complaints until today, when it has become a sizable trading economy. That of China at the end of 2001, in the hope that this would greatly contribute to make it a "responsible international partner", is, rightly or wrongly, deeply regretted nowadays by a number of countries, notably the US.

Finally, the multilateral approach may considerably slow down decision-making, empowering the diffident and making more difficult, in most cases, to reach agreements. This frequently leads to the advocacy of more restrict, plurilateral, regional or thematically based agreements, with an opt-out clause.

In the post-Covid times, multilateralism may experience less demand and have a more restricted range.

Rosenau (2004) proposed a taxonomy for international organisations – or spheres of authority (SOAs), as he calls them under a more general viewpoint, comprising six different types of arrangements, and allowing the inclusion of different actors, as outlined in Section 3.1. Possible outcomes range from the classical, top-down hierarchical institution, found in the Bretton Woods constructs, to a so-called

Möbius-structure. In the latter, cross relationships among different networks of specific actors – transnationals, states, NGOs and others – operate under a flexible scheme which, like the famous Möbius band in mathematical topology, has no inside nor outside, alliances and positions gliding continuously within/along the structure/band, according to the issue at stake, assuring an encompassing view and malleable though effective governance.

The problem with such an original and appealing idea is that ultimately someone has to give orders and see to it that what has to be done is actually accomplished. This "someone" has almost universally been the state: the classical approach is fully centred on it, with more or less than a spice of multilateralism, depending on the institution, to ensure fairness and a minimal voice to the small ones.

If the strategy of multilateralism, with its simplicity and elusive absolute fairness, is neither sufficient nor appealing any more to completely tame the rule of instincts akin to anarchy, other solutions need more elaboration and a clearer assignment of responsibilities.

Multilateralism, still a serious alternative, will remain, but less widespread and more conditioned. It creates viable inter-state communities, provided there does not exist much asymmetry in the established power balance. To believe naïvely that it does abolish the underlying jungle spirits is a childish fantasy: it is merely super-imposed on them. The royal nexus where it should be preserved is the UN, whose lingering reform, as shown by the pandemic, became more urgent.

The blatant heritage of the Holy Alliance or Concert of Great Powers – the best historical analogy is up to the reader, the Security Council, where three main world actors appear among the permanent members, must be adapted to the new realities. France and the UK, which disproportionally shift its representativeness to the so-called "developed Western world", may be partially compensated by the composition of the rotating, elected members, but continue to make for an imbalance hard to be accepted.

Despite the huge task it presents to the world community, there is no option, up to now, outside improving the UN. Moreover, under its broad multilateral stance, it seems unavoidable that China will occupy more space in it. A trend already clear before the start of the pandemic, as described in Chapter 2, that may turn into a fierce competition with the US in the new reality.

As one of the contentions in this book is that reality changed – and Chapter 5 provides a good example of how different actors, in the case transnational information technology companies, want to have a say, one must also start to get acquainted with mixed forms of global governance institutions where decision-making will be the outcome of a more complex process, mixing horizontal and vertical information flows and power balances.

There seems to be no great problem in envisaging an empowered WHO working, for instance, under a multiple mode, combining the classical, hierarchical and multilateral features of the World Health Assembly and its crucial IHR, with network structures, joining academia, research centres, subnational public health institutions to sectors or divisions of the Organisation, in order to deliver more services, at less cost and increased efficiency.

Allowing more room for select members, from China to India, but also Russia, Brazil, Indonesia, Nigeria and other regional powers, may ease tensions, despite the poor and deceitful record of such "concessions" within the Bretton Woods system. Structures that may lead to streamlined, more transparent decision-making procedures including budgetary sources and allocations, either under multilateralism or other institutional designs, will be in great demand by actors beyond the nation states.

The annoying remaining question is whether such a transformative process in the international institutions will be able to make up a consistent reply to the problems left by the pandemic, together with those already existing.

3.3 The forgotten though existing institutions

At the side of visible examples like the WHO and WTO, dozens of international organisations are found, with the great majority of the world community completely unaware of their existence. It is not surprising that every week an idea for a new structure pops up somewhere: an already existing structure ...

Reasons for this proliferation are varied. Sometimes, specific geostrategic concerns, under the guidance of a superpower, motivate the initial endeavour. The OSCE – Organisation for Security and Co-operation in Europe was created in 1975, during the Cold War, and has adequately morphed itself according to the several developments since. With headquarters in Vienna, it includes all European states and the majority of Central European ones, enjoying UN status of a regional institution. In a sign of the power interests behind its creation, it includes the US and Canada, members entirely alien to its focus region. Without denying its good-willed and sometimes fruitful actions it bears clear overlaps with several UN agencies, NATO, the EU and other associations.

Specific global sectors may give reason to other creations. International transport, an area strongly affected by the pandemic, has two flag institutions: ICAO – International Civil Aviation Organisation and IMO – International Maritime Organisation. They should count as key actors in the recovery of the respective activities. Nevertheless, their proceedings and decisions take place nearly in a parallel reality, with relevant stakeholders and interested parties absent, excluded or ignorant of their decision-making.

In 2015, after the nuclear disasters in Japan, during the Third UN World Conference in Sendai, Japan, UN members adopted The Sendai Framework for Disaster Risk Reduction 2015–30. How effective has the Framework been in the Covid-crisis?

Examples could continue, making for a huge cabinet where several scarcely known to unknown institutions, many never heard-of outside of a small circle, are hanging into oblivion. Their governance ended in the hands of a few bureaucrats and specialised professionals; left to fulfil their basic role, at best as an efficient operational agency, alienated from a global governance perspective, draining resources and duplicating tasks.

As stated in the propositions in Section 3.1, *international institutions cannot be more than their members want them to be.* Uncontrolled multiplication leads to forgetting once needed and interesting arrangements, overtaken by other pressing realities and novel government priorities. Often, in the changed context, new actors want to leave their own imprint or peculiar views.

But if people, civil servants, diplomats and priorities change, forced by different political dynamics, most of the problems that motivated the institution do not. Global catastrophes and the Sendai Framework is a telling example: one wonders which role the Framework played during the pandemic.

In the world corona changed, public opinion and international fora will be bombarded with ideas for indispensable pacts, organisations and agreements: nearly all re-inventions or superpositions, consuming funds, time and (hopefully) qualified minds.

Voices calling for a comprehensive review of the present mesh of institutions and agreements would contribute to streamlining the nowadays sick, confusing and expensive international system. The UN would specially benefit from a more transparent, connected and understandable image.

The discussion in this chapter points to a more pessimistic than positive answer. In the short to medium run, states will contend, trying to grab control of institutions, not worried about their reform or improvement. Though weak and in a state of flux, they can be strategic pieces for cleverly reacting to unwanted policies. The two superpowers will vie for some of them, the UN system in top priority. Middle powers must enter stage.

Note

1 This line is strongly supported, with relevant ideas if maybe a trifle optimistic, by many in the Canadian think-tank CIGI – Centre for International Governance Innovation. More balanced views have been exposed by Simon Evenett, for instance, in the international business and trade context.

4 Reaction II

Placing the other countries

4.1 Middle powers: a possible inventory

The performance of the two main rivals during the corona-crisis is not sufficient to allow charting developments in a post-pandemic reality. Since the US failure to tackle its brief moment of absolute hegemony, after the successive falls of the Berlin Wall, in 1989, and the Soviet Union, in 1991, it became evident that other main actors, usually with significant influence either regional or in their neighbourhood, were also determinant in the reshaping of the international order.

This was not exactly a new perception, as countries like India or Turkey, Brazil or Australia – even when playing second fiddle or a complementary role- or an integration project like the EU had always been considered relevant for a number of specific analyses and issues. Moreover, at the side of a more visible emergency of the China-US pair, the greater dispersion of power and the higher interconnections and cross-dependencies created by transborder flows oblige to give more attention to other countries.

Several kinds of data, financial transactions, FDI and value chains exchanges, together with business, professional and academic mobility, nowadays travel in all directions, linking the superpowers to other actors. Select hubs, key sources of activities or their attractors, regional powers or potential ones, such as owners of nuclear weapons, they attenuate the bipolarity. Among further examples, the creation and relative establishment of the BRIC(S), after the Ekaterinburg meeting in June 2009, despite the ups and downs of the group, testifies the need and existing space for such actors, usually identified by the umbrella name of Middle Powers.

Contrasting their behaviour before and during the pandemic can be used as an important signal of how and why a more inner-looking world of less co-operation and sometimes unexpected and hardly

DOI: 10.4324/9781003166726-4

durable alliances may become a reality. In different ways, and with nuances according to the prevailing leadership, each of the two giants would like to gather as many middle powers as possible around its actions, supporting or sharing objectives and burdens, and consolidating a hopefully global influence. The new Biden administration has repeatedly called for the rebuilding of a broad alliance, led through "power and example" by the US. The coming reality, if not showing signs of greater polarisation, seems to point towards a more balanced stance, with smart players changing sides, depending on the issue at stake.

An overview of crucial actors in the main great regions of the world, taking into account the different contexts where they act, may shed some light on the partnership question. Analysis should ideally focus on three key aspects: How and with whom are they more likely to side with? How sustainable will the forged alliances be? Which scope will remain for individual power-projects? As the following lines demonstrate, answers cannot be clear-cut, due to the shifting character of the on-going transformations and the different and sometimes conflicting concerns within each of the two giants. Exogenous innovations and events, triggered by technology and divisive views on the shape of government, democracy and other public governance systems as well, add to the uncertainties.

Before addressing the chosen middle powers, a few words on their global behaviour during the pandemic are important to set the background for the analyses. In overall terms, lockdown policies, demands on the domestic health systems and the varied ways of public reactions around the world, induced a greater introspection within the countries themselves. Broader views or attempts, consistently based on combined action by groupings of nations, were dearly absent. Efforts for the successful creation of a vaccine have predominantly displayed competition rather than collaboration, though some research centres of different origins have associated their capacities and results. Protectionism and heightened nationalism are but two aspects that come hand in hand with such instances and compose a comprehensively more selfish pattern that, depending on its relative strength, will set the background of the New Order.

Southeast Asia

The choice of this region to start the debate is intentional: to call attention to an actor due to become ever more important. It is dominated by the ASEAN, an innovative regional integration comprising the ten economies in the area. Innovative because ASEAN, contrary to the European Experiment, has a much lighter bureaucratic structure and had as main original motivation a desire – as relevant as, or even more than that of deeper economic ties – to build a common security structure. With a flexible design, the Association survived generalised incredulity and many crises to eventually become, last year, the building block of the Regional Comprehensive Economic Partnership (RCEP), signed together with Japan, China, South Korea, Australia and New Zealand. This initiative took more than a decade to be completed and passed through different formats, like ASEAN plus China, or plus China and Japan, and later, plus the first three other Asian economies, in the present partnership.

ASEAN's role, actual and potential, is usually misinterpreted as it is neither a buffer between China and the rest of Asia, nor an unconditional ally or an economic province of the Middle Empire – though less advanced industries and value chains segments are dumped there by it, and Chinese FDI exerts an indirect control of the main economies, nor a promising foothold for the US in the region: to some extent it may play or be all these things. If China trades more with ASEAN than with the US, the Association hosts around 4.200 US companies, and US FDI in Southeast Asia is bigger than its combined amount in China, Japan and South Korea.

The geographically strategic position of the group, containing the key Malacca and Sunda Straits; the existence of Chinese diasporas in countries like Malaysia and Thailand, and in the increasingly Chinese state of Singapore, itself closely tied to the US as regards defence, particularly naval forces; the cultural and economic presence of other Asian middle powers such as Japan and India, which still provide development assistance to the region; and the mesh of economic links with the two giants, in a scenario of sustained growth and attractiveness of a booming consumer market, signal that it will preferably tread an independent path, marked by an overall neutrality towards the two poles.

Broadly, it is geographically, economically and culturally closer to China, but it would be a mistake to include it as a steady ally.

As demonstrated in recent times, it usually adopts a discreet profile, while rising as an unavoidable actor in the region. RCEP is a modest diplomatic breakthrough, well in the style of the Association, despite its failure in eventually engaging India. It puts China and Japan together, at the same time that integrates the "Western representatives" in Asia, namely Australia and New Zealand, each day more dependent on their location.

RCEP is also an innovative venture that contributes to diminish polarisation in the region, without the ambitiously encompassing purposes of the frustrated TPP, which bore a veiled intention of isolating China, and attuned to the kind of economic integration ASEAN itself was slowly and rather successfully implementing among its members. If wisely managed by the ten ASEAN members, it can establish in them a significant common ground for joint activities with the five other partners; something already very good news for the world corona changed.

Simultaneously, RCEP will strengthen ASEAN's economic and political clout in Asia, where 50 per cent of world GDP is generated, making it a more prominent actor not only in the region but also worldwide.

This discussion leads naturally to the related Asian quintet.

India, Pakistan, Japan and the two Koreas

The first two powers possess nuclear weapons, setting them, together with one of the Koreas, in a category apart; both suffered from the pandemic in a way that exacerbated their peculiarities.

India is a key player in Asia and a permanent candidate for a similar position in the world. Economy and population, though through long and winding roads, are almost doomed to grow, and the sheer size of the country makes it more than noticeable. However, serious weaknesses blur the possible extent of its power in this decade, particularly after the pandemic.

The diversity asset, especially as regards the triplet race-culture-religion, has been at risk during the recent administrations, which overemphasise the Hindu component of the society. The endemic dire poverty, inequality and health problems, coupled with a social culture where individualities and argument, for better or for worse, many times prevail over co-ordinated and more pragmatic action – something apparent at all levels, from local administrations to the higher democratic institutions – make progress slower. The attainment of common goals requiring concentrated and sustained efforts – whose importance has been so often evidenced in the Chinese saga – becomes difficult if not sometimes impossible. The result is a giant with still fresh clay feet, hindering a few decisive steps.

On the other hand, this peculiar timing and logic – not akin to either the Western or the Chinese mind – has its advantages and makes it an important piece in many circumstances. Ambiguously autonomous, as brilliantly performed since Jawaharlal Nehru times, at ease with Russia – still an important arms and military technology supplier – and courting the US while separating the dark from the bright side of its complex relationship with China, a global and regional competitor, neighbour in the crucial Himalayan ecosystem, India may offer an alternative, either to China or to the US, to several problems and postures in the international scene.

With its multiple acceptance in different groupings – BRICS, developing countries, Indo-Pacific actor, nuclear power, multi-cultural nation, Africa's friend – it can, with a bit of luck, successfully play the role of an indispensable and reliable partner, with ever-growing international acceptance and clout. The supply of its vaccines to other main countries, like Brazil and big African nations, may greatly contribute to its international goodwill. India will be a key though hardly determinant player in coming times.

A further weakness plagues its near future, something coming from the unfortunate partition of the Raj, in 1947: its relation with Pakistan (and Bangladesh as well). Sharing centuries of history, culture and civilisation, the two neighbours simultaneously lose from poor to dangerously tense relations. India will never achieve a greater power status while held down by the "Pakistan liability"; Pakistan, though pursuing bold and not always clever foreign policies, cannot ignore the close-distant brother without which it also loses status and clout.

The two superpowers, in different moments and through different policies, have tried to attract Pakistan to their side, but the country has proved resilient to a full, steady alliance with any of them. The strategic position of its coast, at the entrance of the Persian Gulf, makes it a natural outlet to the Indian Sea and then the Atlantic for a country like China, bypassing the jammed straits of Southeast Asia. Combined with its four crucial interior borders, it is an invaluable asset. Its well trained and capable elite, and united society only augur better times, if the foreign sector is streamlined and better managed.

Unfortunately, during the pandemic, both countries remained at odds, providing further evidence that improved relations are not to be expected soon. Like India, though not exactly for the same reasons, Pakistan is doomed to clay feet for the time being, as a middle power.

Japan constitutes a different riddle that events like the RCEP and the country's remaining idiosyncratic and successful response to the pandemic might signal the solution. For more than ten years already, it has endured a progressive loss of importance as an Asian power, compounded by an ageing and diminishing population. Still extremely competent in technology and international banking and finance, nearly top in several manufacturing niches, and with a network of ventures, firms, partners, foreign assistance projects and economic interests in the region, even in China where it was a main starter and developer of global value chains, Japan is an undeniable regional power.

Technological prowess enables it to produce nuclear armament, in perhaps a few weeks if needed, though in principle this does not seem a desired outcome. It has been strengthening and enlarging its armed forces, under the excuse of escalating tensions in its surroundings, the South China Sea conundrums being emblematic.

The key question for the Japanese nation in the post-Covid times is until when will it stand as an advanced and to some extent fearsome advanced post, guarding Western, actually US interests and visions in Asia, or will it assume more fully its oriental destiny, deepening ties with all its neighbours and wisely managing a more wide involvement with China? This does not imply a break with the US, even less antagonising it, but certainly nuances the present bilateral relationship, and changes priorities in ways that may be ill-received by the other partner. Given its still considerable technological and financial clout, the time for such a decision is ripe; loss of these two advantages will turn it into a client state, either of the US or of a more assertive China.

The importance of RCEP comes round, as a path to place Japan closer to the other members of the Partnership, opening the doors to a revived immersion in Asia. It is hard to conceive, in the medium to long run, an insulated Japan because of a notional loyalty to the US, when it may rearrange itself as a distant ally with strong and clever ties in its neighbourhood. The post-pandemic context, after the extremely successful and detached performance of the country, may further help to quietly start this significant turn, despite US efforts to keep it in its orbit.

The same applies, at a lower magnitude and with a notable difference, to South Korea. The 1945 division of Korea, which eventually led to the 1953 armistice and the (informal but) effective consolidation of the partition, after the North-South War, still creates strong forces of attraction and repulsion between both halves. The former seems to predominate slowly as evidenced by the recent 2017–9 episodes. North Korea enjoys a curious strategic position, bordering China and Russia and acting as a relevant though not crucial piece in the global chessboard. Yet, it needs its Southern brother and, apparently, there is ground to believe that both parts do want, if not to re-unite, to move towards a closer relationship. It is a decision that implies geopolitical costs for both, but also rewards that eventually surpass them. If Japan changes track to become more embedded in Asia, incentives for this reunion will increase, with Korea – either as a single unit or a friendlier pair – becoming an important match and equivalent regional player.

The above possibility, not at all a certainty, may become more likely if trends previously outlined combine with – as forecasted for ASEAN – a more neutral stance of the Asian middle powers towards the two giants. The economic shift to the area, something continuously strengthened by orientalists such as Mahbubani (2008), aided by the uneven recession that, after the pandemic, Western economies will endure, while their Eastern doubles continue to grow and ascertain the importance of their consumption markets, may be further incentives for a more autonomous joint development.

Undoubtedly, for the four (or five) nations in this heading there is an unavoidable military and security dimension, affected by reorientations like those forecast above. Nevertheless, and here lies a crucial aspect of a wise neutral position, changes may be enacted more as re-adaptations than ruptures, diplomacy playing a fundamental role in transforming, sometimes just turning less intense, the existing alliances.

Will a Mexican standoff be possible, involving China, Korea and Japan, or China, the US and Japan[1]? Beyond other considerations, this sounds less unrealistic in the after-corona times if the US pursues a more aggressive stance, backing Korea in the first triangle, or overtly menacing China, against Japan's interests, in the second, but chances are that the first three countries will become more entangled, leaving the US aside.

Turkey and Iran

These two Islamic countries represent main strains in the development of the Muslim creed. Turkey is broadly a follower of the Sunni line, since the Ottoman Empire times, having been the seat of the Caliphate in its last years; Iran stands as a bastion of Shi'a creed, acting as a focus for its followers in other areas, notably in Iraq, Lebanon and Syria. Both have long and solid historical traditions, Iran displaying a cultural heritage in many ways comparable to India's and China's; both display above average diplomatic credentials, with Iran, in particular, counting with a large number of high-level, some outstanding, diplomats and negotiators.

Middle powers with respectable military power – Turkey exhibits a large active Army, with more than 260.000 people, while Iran touches 350.000, they cannot be excluded from affairs related to the Persian Gulf and the Middle East, and consequently the unavoidable spill-overs on Asia and the Mediterranean. Iran controls the entry to the Persian Gulf, though not entirely, while Turkey the sources of the

Tigris and Euphrates, the main elements of the communications and water supply systems for all countries southwards. Turkey is a buffer state for migrants from the Middle East – fleeing either war or poverty, trying to reach the European Union (EU) soil.

The classic, pre-corona setting opposes Iran and its Shi'a followers to the Sunni or close-to states; demonised by the recent Israeli governments – though not necessarily by the whole elite in the country – it roughly stands as a great nuisance the West would prefer to forget or, for the more radicals, to eliminate. But things are not so simple and there is no assurance at all that, without Iran, the complex labyrinth of the Middle East and the Arab-Israeli dispute would be more amenable; on the contrary, catastrophic scenarios can be easily devised.

The engagement of Iran in a more normal multilateral context will require support from either one of the big two or – what would be another novel outcome – of a representative group of middle powers, in clout and perhaps also in number. The Joint Comprehensive Plan of Action (JCPOA), signed at the end of the Obama II administration, signalled a way to less tense and more productive relations. But the US left the Plan in 2018, and it is uncertain whether it could be renewed, despite existing goodwill from all other signatories.

In a post-corona context, the state of the US-China dialogue notwithstanding, and the sometimes religiously charged character of questions affecting the country, relations might improve. More encompassing demands from the US for re-joining the Plan of Action – as revision of the sunset clauses and, most difficult, of inclusion of Iran's ballistic missile programme – may set limits to such improvement. The novel option above seems more likely: out of regional and also more far-reaching objectives, a set of countries not opposing Iran may contribute to a way out of looming stark isolationism. But this implies an extra degree of co-operation from the very countries in the set, a scarce currency in the new context, probably only mobilised by the intervention of China and, in this case, Russia.

Iran and China have signed in 2020 a draft co-operation agreement. The Chinese, playing a delicate game, are progressively extending co-operation and soft power in the Middle East, ranging from nations in principle opposing Iran, as Saudi Arabia, to closer ones like Iraq, with the divided – in terms of alliances – Gulf States and Egypt in the middle. The technical proficiency of Iran's elite – the country produced its own vaccine for Covid-19 – may benefit from a closer alliance with China, where the country may find an additional, discrete ally for stabilising its economic and political worries.

Will Turkey help Iran in such endeavour? Plagued by unfavourable economic conditions, treating the Kurdish question as a nightmare and surrounded by a perhaps more unstable neighbourhood than Iran's, Turkey pursues a path with no clear destination. Broadly acting as a sort of "distant allies", the two countries share both a *contentieux,* as in Libya and Syria, as well as friends, as Qatar, among diffident Arab countries. It is also interesting to remind that, jointly with Brazil, Turkey had managed to fix a deal regarding Iran's nuclear programme, which was subsequently aborted by Western powers led by the US.

The unavoidable middle power status of the two countries, together with the very complex geo-strategic context where they act, bears no guarantee that they will be able to play a clear, assertive role in the coming order, though they will remain important pieces, especially Iran, for assuring a more peaceful time.

Brazil and Uruguay

South America will not be a region of direct concern; in the coming post-corona times it is hard to conceive, despite the relevance, natural resources' wealth and inherent interest of most of its countries, their having a significant role in the medium run.

Two at least deserve mention, one due to its sheer importance, the other as an interesting counter-example, or rather a complement to the very idea of middle powers.

In the coming renewed environmental debate, independently of how effectual it will turn out, Brazil surely is a main voice and focus of attention, given its status in the global resources pool. This position, shared by only a few other nations, must not be divorced from its increasing role as an international food supplier, rivalled maybe only by the US.

The impact of the top agribusiness-economy activities on the abundant natural resources gives many times way to heated evaluations, additionally confounding an otherwise calmer, if always difficult dialogue, subject to the vagaries of large ecosystems management. The pandemic heightened nationalism nearly everywhere, and under which mood and intensity it will resume in the environmental narrative is strongly correlated to wider political arrangements, ideally involving the UN. Depending on the circumstances, even a stark green advocate, as the EU – despite or thanks to its own internal liabilities – may adopt a more reasonable and enlightened attitude. China, India and select African countries may also play significant roles in how things evolve, though effective alliances should not be much expected.

Moreover, the two qualities above, combined with the size and geographic position of the country – ten neighbours and the longest continuous coastline in the world – create serious security concerns. In a world where nukes are expected to come to the fore, arms race is – discreetly or not – accelerating and national autonomy in terms of basic resources will be considered vital. This will be an additional and costly stress.

Uruguay, a country with about 3,5 million people and a total area of 176.000 km^2, enters stage as a reminder that small powers, in local and also regional terms, may count more than implied by global analyses and forecasts. It displayed a good performance during the initial stages of the pandemic, probably due to a less unequal and fairly civilised population, coupled with a reasonably functioning governance structure. Though the good start deteriorated, health and epidemic control are left under the responsibility of competent technical experts.

Uruguay frequently plays a harmonising role in MERCOSUL – the Southern Cone integration project – in the midst of the giants, Argentina and Brazil, to which its economy is much dependent. With a high-level diplomatic corps and usually clever foreign positions, the country often uses its modest clout in a near optimal way. The result is that its local contribution to regional stability and union is not negligible and will continue to be most needed in the post-corona reality.

Attention should be given to similar examples, in other areas, that may come out as instrumental, depending on the situation or impending conflict.

Russia

Though heavily hurt by the pandemics, but showing its historical resilience, be it in the number of deaths per 1 million people, be it in the forefront of the competition for a performing vaccine, Russia continues to be a major middle power, geopolitically and militarily relevant.

The fact that the Russian Army is perhaps the best trained-on-the ground force in the world, having been in constant, uninterrupted activity for more than a hundred years, together with the country being a major actor as regards nuclear armament and weapons technology in general, makes it a more than significant actor.

It is outside the purpose of this text to review the arguable relationship and related behaviour of the West, notably the US and the EU, with the post-Soviet Union Russia, in the significant unfoldings that were the German re-unification, the NATO enlargement and the not so discreet urge to encompass, if possible, Georgia and Moldavia, together with the two-sided tale of Ukraine, when top EU officials openly encouraged the population to depose a government duly elected. If the EU, out of all this, was and is afraid of Russia, Russia – and very likely correctly – was and is also afraid of the EU and NATO.

Relations grounded on reciprocal fear do not announce constructive outcomes. Aggressive rhetoric, many times from representatives of the US establishment, coupled with a wish-list in which Vladimir Putin is a malignant genius to be disposed of, while the "oppressed Russian people can be redeemed thanks to the attraction of Western values", despite being hurt by blind sanctions imposed on them by the very West, have an undisputable taste of *éternel retour* and do not seem the way to find stable solutions, if any at all. The resilient Russian economy, by diverting imports, cleverly resorting to an import substitution industrial policy and boosting domestic agriculture, has managed to more than survive in the face of continual Western economic restrictions.

The Russian dilemma has two dimensions. First, to assure a minimum breathing space in its surroundings, keeping part of the Soviet remains especially as regards defence and strategic positions: the Crimean affair is an emblematic example of this. In this dimension, there is substantial overlap with European projects, desires, suspicions and fears. Second, in a broader scope, to exert influence – for multiple reasons, strategic as well as cultural and economic – in farther zones, basically Central Europe and the Middle East, where its intervention in the Syrian *imbroglio* has also been emblematic.

The possibility of a more conciliatory dialogue between it and the US, in the post-Covid times, is doubtful, as positions are deeply ingrained and would require a longer horizon to actually change. Its closer associate will become ever more China: the two countries will manage a motley relationship in which closeness will not exclude autonomy and sometimes controlled divergence. It will be easier to align interests with the Chinese power than with the old American rival, in the midst of a complex game in which Asian middle powers like the Koreas, Japan and even ASEAN members will also be involved.

The EU actors will remain divided and mildly assertive, disturbed by other more urgent problems. France and Germany are not necessarily against an improved relationship, the same applying to the Eastern anomalous members, Poland excluded but Hungary certainly in.

Russia will continue to be a major player in Central Europe and in the Middle-East divided stage, and a continuous source of tension – not prone to escalate, though – in the NATO borders. Its good-will during the pandemic, particularly by providing vaccines to Latin American and African (suddenly) forgotten nations, and even to India and the EU, together with the serene way it tackled the epidemic, will be a plus in the near future.

What about the others?

The fact that middle powers like the UK or Canada, or less powerful countries but commanding important resources, significant size or regional prominence, like Argentina, Nigeria, South Africa or Kazakhstan, or a key transition country in the American continent like Mexico, have not been singled out does not mean they will have no influence or should be discarded pieces in the coming order.

Like the butterfly effect in chaos theory, an incident or apparently trivial development in a smaller nation, or in any middle power, may trigger an expanding wave with major and unpredicted consequences. Be it a misunderstanding over Taiwan, with catastrophic consequences for the two superpowers; or a smart soft power policy, like Serbia's efficient and generous management of vaccination, friendly helping neighbours, to the surprise of some, and EU nationals, and establishing a bridge between them and its traditional ally, Russia.

The selection above translates a personal vision on the actors that, in the time span of the present analysis, will, with greater probability, determine the major trends and, most importantly, shift the balance in the alliances they will take part. A country like the UK of course makes a difference if it moves to an even closer association with the US, or sails in the reverse direction, mobilising its still formidable financial, media and intellectual endowments and expertise, but it will not be as determinant as a Russian move, or a Brazilian environmental policy may be. Old continental European powers, such as France and Germany, will be touched in the next section.

4.2 Regional groups, associations and the fate of regionalism in general

As well with individual middle powers, regional initiatives and organisations will re-position themselves. BRICS, the recent African efforts – the encompassing Free Trade Initiative included, the confusing picture in South and Latin America, with nearly a dozen of weak or decadent associations, and the Chinese ventures in Asia, Africa and Central Europe/Eurasia, all will endure transformations and power shifts. The same applies to the post-Brexit-cum-Covid-19 EU.

Despite that some of its key members could well deserve an independent treatment, the EU continues to strive to act as one single foreign power, successful or not, and as such will be analysed. Moreover, its most important country, Germany, is an extremely careful, faithful and strong supporter of the European Project. Having previously discussed ASEAN, as well as three BRICS members, attention will also be given to an important, blurred issue in terms of a precise definition, but relevant in the discussion of potentially powerful associations, diffuse as they may be: the Islamic world.

Before these two specific constructs, regionalism itself deserves a closer view.

From the highly institutionalised format of the EU, to the simpler and flexible one of the ASEAN, or the even looser and non-connected space of the BRICS, to the stalled though still-alive moment of projects initiated under the inspiration of the European model, like MERCOSUL, the existing integration attempts do not seem to come as a priority in the new order. Conditions and incentives have greatly changed, and the economic engine became less unidimensional, more uncertain and intertwined with the technological and standards dimensions, facets that benefit from wider geographic scope. Politics, consequently and naturally, will continue to provide motives for associations, but they are likely to be, for a considerable time, more focussed and restricted.

Rather than integration dilemmas or pursuits, the pandemic has brought forth, or better refreshed public awareness towards big issues that loom over humanity's future. Credible or not, over-stressed or not, climate change and the increasingly encompassing pollution activities, catastrophe management, global health, the transformation of standard politics and the emergence of hybrid systems – illiberal democracy, socially concerned authoritarianism and others – are the new forefront of what matters. To cope with them, or amplify the sound of one's voice, global or regional movements may take place; but they'll have little to do with classical regionalism.

The two giants may be together in one movement, may separately support other nations and experiments or may even be absent: the pungency of the theme, the clever use of the digital galaxy and even a minimal representativeness of the members may help to achieve results otherwise and until recently unexpected.

50 Reaction II: placing the other countries

4.2.1 The European Union (EU)

Despite the efforts and successes of Federica Mogherini, and the experience and world-knowledge of Josep Borrell, the former and present High Representative for Foreign Affairs and Security Policy, respectively, the joke attributed to Henry Kissinger – whom should I call in case I have a problem with the EU? – still applies.

The combination of sovereignty and supranational governance, tested, tried and roughly accepted in the modern existence of the Union, since Jacques Delors' 1985–95 transformative presidency of the EC, still poses problems, doubts and, with an annoying frequency, a waste of precious time. The old cliché of the "democratic deficit", particularly as regards the attributions and engagement of the European Parliament, remains true, despite undeniable improvements, not as encompassing and fast as hoped at the time of the Treaty of Lisbon. The conundrum regarding the existence of a European Army and its rapports with NATO, the NATO-dependence itself, only aggravated by disguised free riding initiatives like France's European Intervention Initiative (EI2), persists. All amidst sometimes Panglossian claims that everything is moving to a harmonious solution, in the best of all possible integration projects.

The plethora of small, medium and huge constraints and contradictions arouses in the external observer a mixed sensation of an always-interesting work in progress, unable to produce a consistent and efficient final image of a main and credible international actor. The vaccines' *melodramma,* poorly managed by the EC mandarins, serves as one of the latest, outstanding examples. Financially, it is an actor anchored by a currency with no common budget and fiscal system, again gingerly moving to the right direction, but always *moving*, never established in a way allowing to include it as a steady partner.

No wonder the Union's voice oscillates among its main members, despite each time more concentrated in Germany; despite continuous efforts by France to prove the contrary; and now finding dissonances in the likes of Hungary, Poland, or even the Czech Republic or Romania. Not to mention the unfortunate "Northern rule-followers" versus "Southern lazy-spenders" divide, artificial and prejudiced, and the often-timid international institutional voice whose main representative still is the Commission.

The EU narrative continues to indulge in statements like "the EU is a project in the making", "the Union comes out ever more robust and integrated after each major crisis", beyond the favoured mantra of "unity in diversity" as key captions, or founding intellectual stones of the project. Nobody denies the stupendous achievements during a mostly successful trajectory started in 1957 at the *Palazzo dei Conservatori*, in Rome, but in a talk about middle powers, the project persistently maintains a consistently *middle* status.

A middle power indeed: a market the size, in nominal GDP, of China's, now and in the near future; a combined defence budget still higher than China's; the weight of its cultural heritage; the quality of a good number of its education and research institutions; the niches of technological competence and the reasonably functioning democracies found in most members notwithstanding, are undeniable qualifications. But a confusing and confused one, lost in bureaucracy, with no clear identity and still looking at the US for guidance and ultimate help, despite individual gestures of autonomy, like the Bilateral Agreement on Investment signed in December 2020 with China.

A power with an ever-promising and ever-diffident persona.

The pandemic gave another demonstration of the hesitant and rather tenuous internal solidarity, overtaken by the search for individual solutions and the actual lack of an integrated spirit. As in the refugee's crisis, the Yugoslav disaster, the Greek catastrophe or the Eurogroup debates, missing solidarity sets the tune. When the reverse is tried, ill-planning, excessive bureaucracy and little internal wars damage an otherwise positive outcome; the whole proceedings related to vaccine procurement are a good recent example, Münchau (2021), the sometimes-pitiful Brexit negotiations another one.

During 2020, an initial rescue package had been produced to alleviate the poorer members. In September of the same year, under the German presidency, an ambitious endeavour, the Next Generation EU, was launched, combining generous grants with a fairly attractive financing scheme. In 2018 prices, the funds borrowed may be used for loans up to an amount of EUR 360 billion, and for expenditure up to EUR 390 billion.

The financial architecture of the package, supported by bonds and financial instruments issued at the EU (budget) level, to be later afforded by new taxes imposed by the members, together with the revenues of a more competitive performance is pioneering. It answers an old desire of correctly starting to operate from a common standpoint, anchored in the Union budget. The programme aims at enhancing competitiveness in the EU realm, targeting the digital and environmental sectors, but lacks the incentive of common pursuits, or of a more co-operative dimension, absent already at the time of its launching. Individual development is promoted, with an indirect when not opaque integration view.

A big unknown exists on the financial feasibility of the whole scheme. A possible development is the addition of an EU-level deficit to the several existing euro-countries' ones, making for a weaker Union, repeatedly crippled in a few key areas and plagued with more political and social tensions. New exits, after the not unsuccessful Brexit result, cannot be ruled out in the more pragmatic times to come; they will make for a hard toll to the integration pursuits.

The increasing US-China rivalry, whether under more polite or aggressive guises, will broadly drive this undefined power again closer to the US. It will fancy with optimally using the two superpowers to its own goals, but will not dare to tread a fully autonomous path. If relevant depending on the issue at stake, the EU will remain, in the coming order, as an ancillary agent, actually more used than using, by both the US and China.

4.2.2 The Islamic world

It may seem odd to include in this section a group so vaguely and broadly defined. However, and at a regrettable cost, core Western powers insist in denying the meaning and importance of this heterogeneous set of nations.

Of the three "religions of the Book", Islam is perhaps the most performing – if one considers the time since its beginning and the speed and geographical scope of its dissemination, beyond exhibiting supple and smart features, like the absence of a – perhaps authoritarian and constraining – main leader, as Catholics have in the Pope, or – depending on the interpretation – the practical and savvy teachings in many of the Koran's verses.

It is a blunt mistake to think or rather dream of an order excluding this enormous, diverse, struggling though ultimately united population going from the mild followers in Indonesia, passing by the many times suffering or persecuted communities in India, China or even Europe, to the variety of beliefs and their institutionalised forms – despite a common threading line – in Pakistan, Turkey, Egypt, Syria, Iraq, Yemen, Saudi Arabia, the Persian Gulf and many major African countries, not to mention the spread of the Shi'a line which has Iran as its flag leader. And beyond all this, the significant Muslim diasporas in the US and the EU, notably in countries like France, Belgium and Germany.

An important modern divide is between those Islamic states which want to separate religion from their business and political strategies, with the United Arab Emirates (UAE) an exponential representative, and those where the union is unquestionable, like the Iranian régime. The developments triggered by the Arab Spring, particularly those in

Egypt, are a good example of how strong these opposing forces can be inside a Muslim country, and how difficult a peaceful outcome can still be.

The present rivalry between Saudi Arabia and Iran is also invoked by some as a fundamental split to maybe worsen in the near future. It would be however hasty to predict deep fractures, as a common bond does exist and the "outside world" influences result, in an algebraic sum, as a factor of union. Besides, concrete gains come from closer and less aggressive mutual relations, as Dubai, with its lucrative ties with Iran, and the UAE recent rapprochement with Qatar exemplify.

During the pandemic, internal and outside rivalries have been temporarily attenuated or forgotten; an issue left aside while the top powers were wrestling with the adequate dose of lockdown and preventive policies to be imposed and the competition to a speedy production of some sort of vaccine. The Muslim galaxy has been accordingly quieter, no paradox, conflict, regret or impasse having significantly progressed.

In the world corona changed, at the side of the US-China opposition an extremely annoying heritage may come back, the lack of comprehensive policies and adequate frames of mind to engage the Muslim world in a common, positive endeavour.

It is an unfortunately naive thought to believe that economic motives will be enough to attract the main Islamic nations: a strategy in which China is becoming unbeatable even among them, while simultaneously realising that it is not enough. A clear, full recognition of their religious identity, which does not necessarily imply acquiescing to all their practices, though requires accepting many, and a way of reconciling their customs with Western ones are pre-conditions to streamline the present latent conflicts, keeping however the identities of both – a dire problem in most EU countries nowadays.

At the side of other main problems, the Islam issue will trouble and condition specific items of the new order, baffling both Western and Chinese policy makers. It may grow to uncomfortable proportions but, before this, the Islamic world will inevitably and deservedly become more assertive.

4.3 Shifting alliances, moving regional interactions

The non-exhaustive list of countries here discussed can be viewed from different perspectives. This text emphasises the idea of shifting alliances as a broad bet that, in the world corona changed, steady alignment to a given superpower, or a key middle power, will be hard to find.

Self-centred nations will care for their own interests and welfare, cherry picking what better suits them in each side. The new US administration will probably be more hectic than China to procure partners in several ventures, from security issues to Tech War strategic moves, safeguarding its own technologies, resources and manufacturing possibilities from the rival and its supporters. But the times will be too fluid and changing to secure such policies for longer times. Pressures and counter-pressures, unfolding in a series of quid-pro-quos – if the West and Taiwan still control semiconductor production, the East, namely China, can restrain access to rare earths – may become frequent and troublesome.

A provocative exercise would be to try to allocate middle powers into categories reflecting their predominant mood in the near future. Imprecise and subjective as it may result, it can shed an additional light to the multilevel chessboard of the coming reality.

India and Russia, and – with nuances – Iran and Japan, could qualify as *independent*, in the sense that they would follow their own agendas seeking superpower support with more than a grain of salt, as their main goal is to ascertain their autonomy and build their own protective sphere.

Australia, New Zealand, Saudi Arabia and even the EU and, to some extent, South Korea could be named *divided*, as they will oscillate more clearly between the superpowers, or one and neutrality or autonomy. The two first ones are more emblematic: irreversibly located in Asia, and highly dependent on their neighbours, they try as best as possible to keep strong links with the US. Intrinsically divided in their alliances and loyalty, they will stick to such a status quo as long as possible – something still feasible in the coming times.

Another group comprises entities for some reason more autonomous, but either not wanting to or being not able (yet) to lead an independent path. They will be courted by both sides, making them *potentially strategic*. ASEAN, Turkey, Pakistan and select African countries are in this group; some, like the first two, may evolve to an *independent* status.

It must be reminded that others may constitute an *ultimately US-group*, in the sense that, in case of a serious divide between the two giants, they will side with the US, even if not under their full acceptance: the context will oblige them. These include parts of South and Central America and, given its multiple facets, the EU itself.

Reaction II: placing the other countries 55

How will the different regions of the world position themselves strategically? It is expected that, like the major and second-level actors, they will try to place themselves at an ideal distance – as a moderate ally, or a fully engaged one, or a neutral entity – in relation to the US or China, but this is neither sufficient nor necessarily an optimal policy. Fuzzy relations, in a world opposing in a nuanced way the big two, as discussed in Chapter 2, may set the tune. Balanced distancing may be impossible, either for regions or for countries, though not moving entirely to full adherence to one superpower seems feasible.

Loyalties and alliances, beyond shifting, will be more diffuse, and attitudes similar to Nehru's India during the Cold War or, if circumstances become more pressing, Finland during roughly the same period, Mouritzen (2017), will be common and perhaps optimal.

Countries like Russia or Turkey – the former an *independent* one, the latter a *potentially strategic* one – will perhaps become more crucial, as if siding with one of the big two, they can, at least *regionally*, turn the odds to their favour. Such "siding", as has been already happening to some extent in the Middle East and the North of Africa, may change according to the issue and related specific interests. Old balance of power considerations seem unavoidable in a less co-operative world, with the two superpowers, like Schopenhauer's hedgehogs, caring to maintain an ideal distance between them.

Pakistan or Indonesia, *potentially strategic* nations differently affected by the pandemic, could try to perform more of a solo act, but the strength of attraction to one of the two poles – already experienced by both – will inevitably prevail, placing them eventually closer to one of them. The same will apply to the Middle East and North Africa region, with more intensity the more dependent on foreign capital and technology the countries will be.

The major unknown in Asia and nearby areas remains India. If moderately hurt by the pandemic, and relatively empowered by a not too negative social-economic outcome, the country, as discussed, may pursue its line of grabbing ever more room and voice in the international high table. If the pandemic turns out nastier, it may instead stand more clearly as a US ally, not necessarily an undisputed one but surely a shield and an opposing force, in principle peaceful, to China. This does not preclude its role in multiple power groupings as previously described, but forces it to be more explicit in a few key areas of exchange and interaction with China – the advantages of which must and surely will be carefully weighed.

The downside common to both options is the already mentioned ever-lasting Achilles' heel: India's unsatisfactory relation with key neighbour (and family member) Pakistan and the domestic poverty reality that, even with a not-so-damaging impact of the epidemic, may worsen both due to it and the international recession, at any level it might attain.

The same applies, in a largely similar way though full of peculiar nuances, to the two key economies in the South China Sea: Japan and South Korea,[2] both alternating between the *independent* and *divided* status.

Despite their fast and clever policies to face the epidemic, both have paid high prices to it, Japan notably, with the postponement of the Tokyo Olympic Games. In a less friendly US-China relationship, even if the US tries not distancing itself from several countries and international initiatives, to the surprise of some, both may eventually tend to positions closer to China's. The recurrent bitter exchanges between the two, which may persist in the new times, may also turn China into a valuable, calmer go-between. Enhancing such a tendency is the slow movement towards closer relations between the two Koreas and the world production core encompassing both and their highly productive neighbourhood, which will continue to gain density with the RCEP. In the background, the strength and duration of the recession provides a further push: the harder and longer it will be, the easier to strengthen ties with China.

The two large, remaining masses, Sub-Saharan Africa and Central and South America,[3] will play at most a subsidiary role for the moment. The former may ultimately result, in relative terms, less affected by the pandemic, according to a few studies, largely due to its favourable – in this case – age pyramid, and the robustness of a population already immune to many health hazards it must daily face.[4] Even if this is hopefully the case, once normality resumes, WHO's troubled and debatable condition will impose a side cost to Africa and the several health initiatives through which it helps the continent. A recession – in any of the two levels assumed here – will severely affect the economies in the region, quite a few dependent on fossil fuels' exports, Angola, Gabon and Nigeria standing as major examples.

Interesting and game-changing initiatives, like the ambitious African Continent Free Trade Area, may provide a positive co-operation drive. It is hard to see the countries in the region siding with one or other foreign power, super or middle. Regional alliances look more feasible, either to help in the economic recovery or to fight a re-emergence of terrorism; if not successful, they risk being stalled, as mentioned at the start of Section 4.2.

But the political and security aspects will also be at risk. About 12 countries had important elections scheduled for 2020, and many have been postponed. The economic difficulties brought about by the recession may change a significant number of political scenarios, with social inequalities and injustices coming again to the fore. The unfortunate growing clout of former ISIS – nearly expelled, for all practical measures, from the Middle-East – will then receive renewed support in the region, and instability and violence are doomed to increase, as already noticeable in territories of Mali, Niger and Chad – with significant spill-overs in Nigeria – the Maghreb, the African Mashreq, Somalia and Mozambique, among other areas.

Without international support, it is trying to imagine how recovery will be achieved in Africa, as the generalised uncooperative mood of the developed economies is likely to provide cosmetic aid to the huge problems to come. This will strengthen China's role in the continent, together with secondary players like Turkey and India, and perhaps, in limited and targeted actions, Russia. The much-deserved African emergence, to occupy a role in the international scene compatible to its resources, size and prospective importance, will have to wait for at least one extra decade.

Regarding the two Americas south of the Tropic of Cancer, together with Mexico, they were already in a state of flux before the pandemic. The last CELAC – *Comunidad de Estados Latinoamericanos y Caribeños* – meeting testified this, and all countries will suffer from the recession and worsening inequality. Many important ones, like Argentina, Brazil and Mexico, were already enduring, in 2019, economic hardships in varying degrees and politically sensitive contexts; negative factors only to be exacerbated in the aftermath of the pandemic.

Lack of a common co-ordinating authority or reliable institution, with the previously mentioned failure of CELAC, with Argentina driving apart from MERCOSUL and the old sick man of the Andes, the Andean Community, having missed a few years ago another opportunity for a revival, while Venezuela and Bolivia still cope with the remains of the Bolivarian attempt, make joint endeavours difficult, if not impossible. No diplomatic leadership is foreseeable either, with national foreign offices mostly adopting more inwards views to mend the damages corona inflicted.

The overall prospect is that, as pointed out with respect to Brazil, this large part of the globe, extremely well endowed with natural resources, will become less relevant, and a clear prey to select interests by China and the US. The attractiveness of its resources and of several potential business and FDI opportunities – in infrastructure and connectivity, for instance – will guarantee a minimal voice to its main economies, but their role as rule-setters, and not merely takers, or even as a desired partner, in the order corona has changed, will be dictated by the cold arithmetic of power.

Notes

1 The Mexican standoff, a concept originally from game theory but appearing in business disputes and even gangster movies, applies when each adversary enjoys a lethal advantage towards at least one of the others, in such a way that, if not stopped by an external reason, the situation leads to the extinction of all involved. It can take place between two, three and actually any number of adversaries, being usually analysed with three or four.
2 Taiwan and Hong Kong are not dealt explicitly in the present analysis not because they are found irrelevant, but of second order for the general discussion here conducted.
3 No detailed attention will be given to Eurasian core nations, for reasons similar to those in the previous note.
4 Given their poor sanitary and health conditions, many Africans are already survivors, having a better equipped and stronger immunological system, in comparison to that of an average European welfare-citizen. This contentious point has been raised by some as an additional explanatory variable for the incidence pattern of Covid-19, at least up to the last quarter of 2020, in the continent. Comparisons between Africa (or Africans) and other groups may be found, for instance, in 'The Global Impact of COVID-19 and Strategies for Mitigation and Suppression', 2020, London: Imperial College, of about the same period. The whole idea is debatable and needs more support; time will say if it really applies. Nevertheless, the argument by no means implies that sanitary and health conditions in Africa do not need to be greatly improved.

5 A main issue and a major example
The digital complex

5.1 After the pandemic: the New Digital?

Perhaps nothing has gained more prominence and been more exploited, penetrating diverse activities and services, than the digital complex. The suppression of physical meetings and their replacement by webinars and several forms of online direct communications, the resort to different delivery systems for providing at home nearly everything from food and meals to medical services under safer conditions and the use of targeted software – the applications or apps – affording multiple facilities and specific tasks increased exponentially. Pundits foresee a significant contrast between a pre-pandemic world, when the digital advanced at an elusively controlled speed, and a post-pandemic one when, thanks to the encompassing role briefly described, a reality completely dependent and orchestrated by an overwhelming digital galaxy will come into existence.

To many, this evolution was already on track, and the contribution of the pandemic has been merely to heighten its acceleration and to amplify the pervasiveness of the process. As for the latter, there seems to be general agreement that the intensified use of the digital as alternative for the absence of personal contact in several activities was somehow unexpected, forcing a replanning not only in middle to big organisations of such variables as office space, modalities of home office, the need of many kinds of meetings and their traditional formats and that of travel for direct interactions among people in separate locations.

At least for business purposes, travelling will suffer a considerable reduction for some time to come, particularly as regards long and short haul flights. Reductions in the former will deeply affect the international oligopoly of the main carriers, and even provoke rearrangements in the domestic markets, already suffering from the lower

DOI: 10.4324/9781003166726-5

internal demand for the latter. Other examples abound, as in the already changing press and media world, where the situation created by the lockdowns and the generalised fear of contacts – even with a physical newspaper! – gave the digital a major boost.

The number of changes can be vast, that of the corresponding forecasts also. Certain questions remain subject to much speculation: the substitution rate between the "normal or traditional" way of performing several tasks and the digital one; and how much of the "old habits and formats" will return, when the pandemic comes under control and physical contact becomes less restrained. Using the idea of elastic and inelastic changes introduced in Chapter 1, most of those brought about by the digital will probably be inelastic, with specific areas, as business practices such as webinars and home office hours, showing moderate elasticity.

It is not the intention in this chapter to dwell on these complex and important exercises, but rather to address broader issues, made cogent by this very predicament. Two major problems, one already debated for at least a few decades, the other more recent, deserve initial attention.

The first is the much-vexed question on the actual contribution to major societal problems and aspirations, like inequality reduction and greater individual freedom, that the digital complex has made. Without getting into specific aspects of each different achievement – if all of them really took place – the global view in this book is that, as an undeniable reality, the digital evolution brought ever more control over society.

Each individual, citizen, consumer of goods and services, financial agent or medical subject became, to a large extent, known to the system as a whole; meaning that, the state first, digitally equipped providers of goods and services second, and then main applications and specific software like the powerful global search engines – have, in varied levels of precision, a chart on and power over him. Whether this contributes to reduce inequality or increase a citizen's freedom is extremely debatable, individuals being much more constrained by the information mesh encapsulating them and less able to pursue independent action or tread unconventional, not necessarily illegal, paths.

Powerful and developed states, China first, followed suit by the US and with close images in the UK or the Scandinavian countries for instance, where the smaller population makes things much easier, are creating a sophisticated, ultra-Big Brother society. Manifold digital tools and devices are replacing different means of social and commercial interactions, ultimately money itself. In China, the data bank related to the individual can in principle feed a scores system, which will immediately rank her position in a "model citizen" scale, with uses in the least questionable. No one doubts that in the US and other Western nations the same takes place, even if in a more discreet and still less encompassing way.

At the side of the states – independently, though oftentimes working with or for them – the big digital platforms have acquired unimagined power. The five Western (US) giants – Amazon, Apple, Facebook, Google/Alphabet and Microsoft – like their Eastern (Chinese) counterparts, as Baidu, the Ant Group-Ali Baba Ecosystem (of firms) and Tencent, are increasingly able to exert control on varied aspects of social and personal life. The market value of the US mammoths rose by 46 per cent during the pandemic, in 2020, reaching 7,2 trillion US$. Moreover, through foundations and philanthropic endeavours, fully funded by their enormous profits, they can mobilise encompassing campaigns and world projects advancing, even if indirectly, their private goals.

From different perspectives, this problematic has already been fairly well discussed in the literature and the press; Crouch (2004), Flôres (2020) and Wallerstein et al. (2013) being a few examples where it composes major, broader arguments. An early warning was McPhail (1987)'s, where the vision of "electronic colonialism" was anticipated.

Two main consequences are worth emphasising.

One is that a social malaise, sometimes hard to frame, is pervasive in modern societies. Bearing interactions with usually negative perceptions on local and state governance, often nurtured by authoritarian measures and implementations by governments, it contributes to the present crises in Western-styled democracies and political systems in general.

The crises are also compounded, though many forget or deny it, by the continuous grabbing of one's mind that the digital environment performs. At the same time that the "world at your hands, through a few touches or by sliding the screen" half-illusion is provided, it alienates, uniformises and disrupts other forms of culture and knowledge acquisition, making room for a society with ironically less diversity and a horde of apps-addicts relying solely – either for fun, or information, or education, or whatever guideline is needed – on their personal device(s).

The other is that power nowadays necessarily includes the ability of creating, managing, implementing and distributing – as widely as possible – the algorithms needed for hundreds (thousands?) of digital tasks. Algorithms that in their turn require sophisticated designers:

people with deep specific skills in the likes of mathematics, natural languages and artificial intelligence methods and procedures, which pre-suppose a modern, high-level educational system. And all this demands time and funds. The result is that, despite the possibility of small, local developments, key and large parts of the digital galaxy and the continual production of algorithms are unequally distributed in the world. The top powers, China and the US, reverting to questions addressed in Chapter 2, are in the sustained leadership of such endeavours, while manifold nations trail behind them, including significant middle powers.

The second problem is of a more general nature, and refers to where is this exponential and intrusive growth of the digital galaxy leading the world society. How will the ever closer and human-like interactions among algorithms and machines unroll, as regards the interfaces with human beings and their influence on multiple activities that up to recently laid outside their interference, Bostrom (2014), Tegmark (2018)? Will this enhance the aforementioned control dimension of the digital sphere, with control itself progressively assumed by the machines? or will this redistribute power in society and the global community, eventually creating unexpected outcomes in the world order itself?

Answers are still to a large extent speculative, and disputed by experts and a few progressive entrepreneurs. They are usually concentrated on the technical or local impacts of the main expected developments – for instance, all implications of a driverless car – and rarely address those on the international order.

The pandemic impacts have contributed, if one can use this word, more to the first point but, as seen below, they have also intersections with the second one.

5.2 Dependencies, impacts and riddles

Reactions, counter-measures, technical and legal efforts are present in every context related to the digital, many times trying to constrain developments, answer or minimise criticism, as those in the previous section.

The security and privacy issues, at the individual, firm, community or national levels, are the object of plenty of proposals and concrete legislation in Western Europe, the EU and other middle powers like Brazil, and will be tackled later. Efforts towards open software and ways to widen access to devices and facilities that would encourage independent production and developments have borne interesting fruits and are being pursued.

A major example: the digital complex 63

The significant push the pandemic gave to the digital and the spreading uses it has encouraged, when not enforced, substantially increased the dependence of whole societies on the digitally supported alternative. The development and ownership of encompassing core systems has become more crucial, and demand for them, since long, has not been fulfilled by independent, small ventures.

As a corollary to the remarks on the unequal distribution of the power to create and distribute major algorithms, oligopolistic structures are already present either in the fields of search mechanisms or in those of the so-called social media – both not unusually combined in a single "platform owner". This concentration movement was originally due to the ungoverned, fast expansion of the internet, which took flight during the second mandate of President Clinton, Tharoor and Saran (2020).[1]

A similar pattern will sprout in several other main digital applications and services. It is no wonder that the new webinars and generalised chats apps show already this feature, with big software producers and search mechanisms owners supplying the most competitive ones. This is expected to continue in nearly any area the object of a reasonably stable demand, many associated with the lifestyle corona has changed. More concentration of power and dependency on the Masters of Algorithms, Valladão (2014), will ensue.

Concentration processes and their consequences, usually adverse to the poor, small or weak, are common to capitalist developments, largely triggered by technological innovations coupled with new, usually loose, market regulations and costly access. Many stories and examples exist, ranging from the revolutionary transformations in agriculture[2] to bold market opening and enlargement measures, like the Europe 92 initiative, pursued in the early 1990s under Jacques Delors, or the more recent GVCs phenomenon.

Without discussing how inevitable each of these processes might have been, and the related value they might have added to, or *extracted* from society, Mazzucato (2018), the aim here is to stress their common pattern and outcomes.

Taking the example of the agricultural sector, it is enlightening to notice that at the side of classical analytical works on the mutations it endured, Hopkins and Puchala (1978) or Friedland et al. (1991), the text by Sen (1981) unveils another side of the process. It introduces the interesting concept of (loss of) entitlement (by the poor, to grow food or earn money to buy it) to explain why, despite increases in the world production of food, hunger became more widespread, notably in the South.

Loss of entitlement to freedom, to autonomy or to ways to avoid bowing to apps-dominance, whether desirable or not, is more than a key issue deserving attention in the new reality: it is a concrete threat. Where will the owners of the new digital apps be found?

In the US and China first and foremost, due to their dynamic technical expertise and competence, together with the priority and funds given to high-tech education and research. But also, thanks to a cumulative effect, because – as mentioned above – while the former hosts all the capitalist giants in the sector, the latter – not forgetting the mix of state and private ownership – displays a considerable constellation of firms ranging from big ones, as their US counterparts, to smaller and very performing ventures, focussing on specific applications.

Countries like India, South Korea, Russia or Germany, among others, may come up with innovations, but it is hard to conceive them as fully autonomous market actors. Those in the European realm would probably fix associations with US firms, or even China, in the case of Germany. Russia, apart from military applications, would eventually have to partner with another power.

During the pandemic, several algorithms directly involving the citizen, something already common in China, were used, like those controlling one's contacts with infected people, or the respective identities of those present at a supposed moment of contagion. Apps for monitoring vaccination or other mass procedures, or the health status of someone, were made popular. Switching such devices to other features of daily life is reasonably simple, must be anticipated and will add to the control dimension of the digital galaxy. Entitlement to freedom and full citizenship will continue to shrink.

But dependence has another side.

Everything in the digital realm requires due telecommunications media to smoothly operate, be it via diverse electromagnetic wavelengths or optical fibres. Proper ancillary devices and protocols, ever more important and specific given coming sophisticated uses like the internet of things, play also a role.

In the long discussions on telecoms services liberalisation, from the mid-1980s to the mid-1990s, along and after the Uruguay Round, it was already clear to be nearly impossible to separate the service itself from the devices and respective protocols. Any trade in services dispute in the area had a dual trade in goods one. A two-sided riddle applies: the apps concentration goes hand in hand with a devices' one, in its turn heavily dependent on technological edges and the new services themselves, in continuous circularity. The much-publicised 5G dispute, where barriers are enforced to equipment, or rather the telecom technology, in order to block the apps and the signal, is a model example of this: the Tech War naturally morphs into a trade in goods war.

Both sides – equipment and signals – rely on a steady and ever-increasing provision of energy which becomes twice more essential than before. The power demand of a single application may be negligible, but the repeated and simultaneous use of a plurality of them, by millions of users, introduces a significant load in the supply systems. Moreover, heavy data processing required by artificial intelligence procedures and blockchain computations is a well-known huge energy consumer.

A power blackout or a failure in a communication channel may lead to disruptive, unthinkable consequences.

Adepts of the "smart cities" idea as well as dwellers happy to perform "everything from home", something heightened by the lockdowns, are many times unaware that a simple hiccup in energy supply leaves them totally disconnected to the whole world, defenceless and at a loss. A situation that reminds, with due respect to the interpreters of the Talmud, the fascinating and intriguing passage in the Torah, stating that "the omission or the addition of one letter might mean the destruction of the whole world".

Optimists may claim that decentralised, ultimately individually based power sources, combining, for instance, solar energy panels with advanced storage devices – expected from the fast evolution in battery technology – may strongly nuance a catastrophic blackout scenario, at least as regards the digital needs. But the nation- or region-wide supply grid seems uncontroversial in the short to medium run. Its central importance is accordingly heightened by the several mass-based, nationwide interventions and campaigns, like vaccination, that will become more frequent in the post-corona world: as state's digital-dependence increases, security of national energy grids may dominate other concerns.

The encompassing mesh of electromagnetic waves in a given location is the ideal background for the scenario denounced by many, the iconic Edward Snowden in particular, in which all devices, if not completely turned off, are continuously scanned and hacked by several unknown signals, invaders and information gatherers. Greater insecurity is added to the manifold data bases associated with the individual. In this setting, security and privacy issues submerge in an ocean of diversified and often conflicting interests mixed with fierce business competition.

While data protection in general has received great attention from several governments, with the EU and Brazil issuing broad-based legislation, in some ways pioneering, defence-related aspects move on muddier grounds. Apart from simple, basic procedures, cybersecurity is mostly viewed as a subject for nations and large corporations; the individual itself does not matter. Even for economic agents in general, the "misalignment of incentives" pointed out by Nye (2011) still matters: the will to provide for their own security is limited by the competitive pricing of their products. In the case of firms, large ones included, there is a financial incentive in not disclosing attacks or intrusions that could damage the firm's credibility, and that of its products or services, making reliable data for designing security measures a scarce good.

It is thus not difficult to expand the geographical scope of such a messy and vulnerable environment, touching again questions of power, competition and fragility among nations.

China and the EU, since 2018, have imposed tougher data protection and transfer regulations; the US Department of Defence has developed concepts justifying extraterritorial cybersecurity operations against alleged cyber-aggressors, such as Iran, North Korea and Russia. The aggressive US stance against the Chinese 5G technology, offered by Huawei, is also grounded on this rationale: it will place key information from business, institutional and private users resorting to Huawei products in the hands of Chinese intelligence, *and so extraterritorial action is required*.

The practical consequences are twofold. First, under the Clean Network Initiative, the US has been extorting the proscription of the Chinese technology from all countries bearing any relationship with the States. Despite a debatable success, its clout and not exactly subtle arguments make for a growing number of signatories of MoU's with such commitment. Second, beyond the devices and protocols, competition has reached the area of technological inputs. Semiconductors are the fundamental piece in all 5G equipment, and they still make for an Achilles Heel to China. Beyond the US, top designers are found in the Netherlands and substantial production takes place in Taiwan; their behaviour is under US surveillance. Tougher competition of this sort, essential to achieve dominance in the digital galaxy, is a sure event in the post-corona times.

Regulation of the digital realm, already backwards in terms of the technical and social realities *before the pandemic*, will thus continue to occupy centre stage in many global discussions, raising once again questions on the need of new international institutions to handle the different aspects of the problem. The International Telecommunications Union (ITU) should be the basic focal point for such efforts, something very reluctantly accepted by the US, though broadly supported by China. The modest trials up to now yield evidence of the fractures between both positions and objectives: one may not proceed in the post-corona order.

Different proposals will continue to be aired but the gist of the hard questions, like nearly all in the digital complex, is tied to higher interests and political decisions, as the ones in the Tech War between the superpowers, and in the adherence to and fate of the multilateral institutions. Fragmentation of the galaxy into a set of digital nebulae – in a line similar to Chuanying (2020)'s "cyber islands" – is a likely solution, depending on the evolution of the US-China relationship.

5.3 A plethora of other issues: which role in the reallocation of power and alliances?

In technology in general, and more intensively in the digital applications with artificial intelligence techniques, to nearly every civilian use of a new device or service corresponds a potential military application, and vice versa. Drones are a good modern example, with multiple uses suitable to both war or peaceful purposes.

The much deeper digital penetration in society after the pandemic will open ajar the door to closer interactions among the military and civilian powers, with the greyish security entities in-between. The impact and influence on the polity may bear unfortunate outcomes.

From an international perspective, this is not the only big question linked to the digital complex. The substantial changes in the patterns and practices of the labour force, where the already increasing automation coupled with the current realisation that presence is, for many tasks, less crucial than previously thought, will bring forth movements of skilled and non-skilled labour, similar to the recent migration flows.

A glimpse on the figures can be obtained from the surge in unemployed in the US, at the beginning of the pandemic in 2020, from 300.000 people to 30 million in about three weeks.[3] Though recovery and new placements have taken place, a sizeable fraction of the higher value is due to the increase in digitally anchored practices and services. Part of this contingent will have difficulty in finding a job, not to say an equivalent one.

Though migration will be mostly regional or even domestic (in large countries), some will also acquire a wider international dimension. Like the "brain drain", or the diverse moves of those excluded from the agrarian sector, or the nowadays Middle East refugees' question, they will shatter the stability of a few countries, often weakening them, while strengthening those able to offer profitable opportunities for the qualified migrant.

The labour argument will be reminded and reinforced, as the ensuing recession due to different closures and stalls in the productive complex will put job creation as top priority. But not only the labour factor will suffer and induce changes.

The pandemic has sounded an alarm on the unending trend of production fragmentation and the creation of global, in the sense of international, value chains. Such a trend had started to be questioned a few years before, due to the ever-present criticism of unfair export of jobs – recently reinforced by more nationalistic policies – but also, and equally strongly, by concerns over the reliability of key production lines. This has been made more acute recently, when in the poorly co-operative environment that prevailed, authorities realised they were unable to manufacture essential things, like certain types of medicine or hospital and medical equipment, many tied to GVCs out of their control.

Ironically, many digital innovations that contributed to the spread of the GVCs phenomenon are also suitable to help in the rebuilding of domestic or more regionalised value chains. Information related to each of the required tasks, their linkages and final assembling lies already in clouds and, but for a specific raw material or physical good needed as input, production became portable and may come back as easily as leave.

This in no way implies that GVCs are doomed. At least in the foreseeable future, their presence in a multiplicity of sectors, their high and near optimal performance and their dependence many times on natural resources only found in certain countries guarantee the continuity of quite many of them. But a rebalance to an extent still difficult to guess, though heavily supported by the digital, will take place. Reshoring of basic chains by big and some middle powers may happen, while other countries may become more open and diversified, to increase robustness of supply; an issue further elaborated in the next chapter.

The financial system, like the press and media sector, has accelerated the pace to eventually turning all its transactions digital, with many countries, from Brazil to China, seriously considering the digital version of their respective currencies. China has indeed made a soft launch of the Digital Currency Electronic Payment, or "digital yuan" as it has been informally called. Apps and other similar facilities, by reducing costs and labour, are making room for the emergence of smaller firms, dedicated to a reduced but profitable set of operations, which are starting to impact several financial markets.

The fiscal area of many countries, always eager for revenues, reacted to the unbridled power and profits from major Western players like

Google, Facebook or Amazon, by opening a legal battle to tax these mechanisms on a national basis, given their undeniable ultimate commercial character. In the EU, programme Next Generation EU, an ambitious effort to reinforce competitiveness and recovery of the economic sector in the Union, will be partially financed by new taxes on digital transactions, to be imposed on an EU-wide basis. Worldwide, with disputable success, and mobilising top law experts in both sides of the dispute, advances from the side of the national governments are taking place.

This question is doomed to become both more visible and engaging, given the deficits many countries will incur due to the subsidies and support measures for coping with the pandemic. It will bring to the fore a conflict that until now had been fought mostly behind law courts by top executives and civil servants: the clash between national governments, or rather national bureaucracies and representatives of the big masters of algorithms, who, not infrequently, claim to represent an advanced, more open and globalised society.

How will this affect the reallocation of power among the actors discussed in the three previous chapters?

A new one has clearly entered stage: the big platform owners, software producers and providers. With similar purposes both in East and West, but important differences regarding their relation to established governments, they will help forging or disrupting country alliances and, heightening a trend already in progress, try to influence targeted international organisations.[4] Platform diplomacy, running in its own track, independently of the official foreign relations lines, will be a new, active reality.

A sounder and more encompassing answer must then start at the level of the individual. He will be subject, all over the planet, to the following impacts, due to a mix of digital developments – most already in course – and the experience of the pandemic:

i   as a member of the labour force, he will stand in a much riskier and more unstable position, calling for increased attention and the awareness that all of a sudden he may become a useless or, if chosen either by him or others, a forever-idle piece of the system;
ii as a consumer, she will be much more controlled and hostage to a variety of oligopolies, some holding a complete record of her preferences, shopping patterns, habits and – maybe indirectly – purchasing power and financial clout. Part or the whole of this information may be passed to government authorities and institutions;

70   *A major example: the digital complex*

iii as a citizen, he will become more constrained and controlled by the State in a way that information on his activities and belongings, his varied interactions with the Leviathan and all kinds of public systems will be easily crossed, contrasted, compared and evaluated; his privacy will significantly decrease;

iv   as a mind and supposedly autonomous entity, she will be massively exposed to a uniform, blinding and usually biased-towards-specific-objectives culture, in an information environment peopled by fake news and largely controlled by media providers, linked to powerful trusts and interest groups in conflict among themselves.

It is this individual who will now be the member of a nation that in principle will face close to savage international competition, in a struggle where, from the digital viewpoint, it will eventually either become a master of algorithms or a client, sometimes a servant hung on a major designer and high-technology supplier elsewhere. An individual morphed into a living object, subject and information good for the big platforms.

Will all this be passively endured?

Pushing somewhat the scenario further, everything in a dependent nation, from its army to the organisation of its public services, from the main goods and services offered to the ability to process and analyse information, will rely on apps and algorithms, and so ultimately on their outside provider.

Differences within the nations and their ability to be master or client will be largely explained by how skilled and autonomous a significant fraction of their societies will be. The previous sentence may seem a rephrasing of an old lesson from development theory that education is perhaps the main factor for change and growth. Nevertheless, without denying the amount of this basic truth, the situation presents relevant twists.

What is now at stake is a transformational technology affecting lifestyles, every main sector of activity and the political system itself; providing opportunities for manipulation, mass control and opinion building, mobilisation and counter-mobilisation techniques. In synthesis, a technology able to choose the way opinions and voices will be heard in, standard democratic or not, governance systems in which the people must somehow take part. It lies at the heart of the Tech War, and affects not only excellence and leadership in manufacturing and services, but financial and military capabilities as well.

As analysed above, it brings in its bosom transnational private agents that may be equally or more powerful than states. Contrary to the classical multinational firms, their alliance to the "home country" is more footloose and they own a technology with over-riding scope and utility, portable and needed everywhere, experiencing no East-West or North-South divides.

In sum, the educational effort that may influence the reallocation of power mentioned above imposes strong alliances between governments and the respective communities in their jurisdiction. Conflicts of interest, predatory behaviour and the allure of more independent pursuits, both by Western and Eastern middle powers, may render less reliable and stable this desired outcome. It is not an enlightening, horizon-opening education that is at stake; rather an extremely targeted one, to produce brains focussed on the various skills that discriminate a master of algorithms from a bare user of them.

The digital complex, in the post-pandemic order, will contribute to diminished citizenship, more restricted individuals and an increasingly competitive, hierarchical order in which, alongside people, the machines will ultimately count.

At the side of education, civil engagement can be an equally balancing and game-changing force. Greater awareness of the new reality will bring more civil participation; counter-reactions may ensue. Wise politics and policies will be dearly needed.

Notes

1 An enlightened critical account of key, historical developments in cyberspace, under an international relations perspective, is found in Chapter 4.
2 Initially triggered by the introduction in the US, in the middle 1920s, of tractors and soybeans, until the present one, of transgenic and huge crops, managed by sophisticated digital systems and machines.
3 Data from 'Unemployment Rates During the Covid-19 Pandemic: in Brief', report R46554, updated January 12, 2021, by the US Congressional Research Office. I'm indebted to Andrea Renda for drawing my attention to this guess, as well as to elements for other arguments in this chapter.
4 See Chapter 3.

6 Outlining scenarios
Dynamic sketches, detailed analyses

6.1 Building blocks

At present, Covid-19 has provoked a significant change in the lives of nearly everyone in the Western Hemisphere, together with sensible effects in China, India and other parts of Asia and the Middle East, as well as looming disruption and varied social problems in Africa.

Besides the enormous difficulties that the dynamics of the pandemic poses and will still provoke, a global though uneven recession is certainly among the major ones. Denied by many, who do not want to heighten the already top levels of anxiety and pessimism, the combination of staggering lockdowns and the likely decrease in overall productivity and trade will inevitably lead to hard times. Some, invoking authors as Scheidel (2017), claim that, ironically, the immediate post-corona scenario can be an opportunity to change the course of the world economy towards a less unequal one. Perhaps, but only after more trouble and strife.

A key though somewhat rhetorical point is whether the whole episode can be considered as a huge catastrophe – like the natural ones, a tsunami or an earthquake, after which the goal is recovery and reconstruction in order to resume normal life as soon as possible – or whether the extent of damage and probations inflicted on different segments of society, and the corresponding behaviour of the nations involved and their respective leaders will not displace for good the references, patterns and perceptions that characterised and shaped the world before the pandemic.

Signs of conflict, international tension and even disarray were already evident before the overwhelming new reality brought by deaths, ignorance, mistakes and fear settled in. It is fair to suppose that the huge impact of the damages will accelerate processes and distortions that were latent, together with new ones, that will irrevocably dislodge the world order to new (dis)equilibria, perhaps far from the previous status quo, unstable as it were. No, the pandemic, also by its duration, cannot be compared to a huge earthquake.

A major evolution is the crises and chaos many regimes are undergoing, from the large democracies like the US and Brazil, where citizen's polarisation is causing unexpected consequences, sometimes surprising and unfortunately misinterpreted as domestic terrorism, to developments like those in Hungary or Poland, different between them and from the revival of Hindu nationalism in India.

In all these contexts, ample dissatisfaction with the status quo, together with a blind reaction from the established powers, fuels a continuously tense domestic environment. It is hard to believe that this will diminish.

Though no room has been given to a full discussion on the already-mentioned, coming economic recession – a recession that might reach levels not far from those in the 1930s, in the past century, if a bad turn occurs – its existence has been taken for granted in Chapter 1. It will be used in the following arguments according to two degrees: a hard one, with significant effects on the US and (perhaps minor) China, and various negative spill-overs on most parts of the world; or a tough but less encompassing and nasty one, naturally and differently affecting the US and China, and many parts of the world as well, but leaving some countries with milder impacts, and giving room to patchy local booms and recoveries around the end of 2021.

These two loosely defined possibilities will interact with other components of a world scenario. Separation of the economic details from the remaining broad geopolitical aspects seems convenient in a first step of analysis, in order to give pre-eminence to main geopolitical features that will shape the world order. The great challenge is to put all relevant elements together in a feasible dynamic scenario.

6.2 Adding actors and problems

Alliances will also be influenced by the planetary interests and roaming power of large corporations, with multilateral institutions sometimes having an ancillary capacity to condition and regulate outcomes. As discussed in Chapter 3, they will broadly continue in a state of corrosion by multiple agents, questions and unsolved issues. The less co-operative Covid-reality is a moment when they are most demanded, while ironically their usefulness remains debatable. Joint actions and geographically comprehensive endeavours are a necessary

74   *Dynamic sketches, detailed analyses*

condition for coping with the borderless problems that will plague most countries; a great unknown exists whether they will be feasible.

One of the main proposals in Chapter 3 is that efforts and funds should be massively directed to the UN, whose lingering reform, as shown by the pandemic, became more pressing. There is little scope for changes in the short run in the Security Council, what, the need to strengthen the UN notwithstanding, may alienate the Council from certain issues and decisions, circumscribing it to a role not much different from the present one. The void will forcefully be occupied by different players, depending on the problem at stake, from regional pacts to plurilateral ententes, not forgetting solo actions by the US or China: the multilateral approach will descend one more step.

The open question of violence and aggressive international behaviour may create trying situations in the New Order, many probably managed by a combination of threat and conciliation by the two superpowers. The pre-Covid state of flux in this area will worsen, generating additional noise to the world order and indirectly – and again – fuelling more power to either the US or China.

Once control is regained and global fear lowers, past unresolved problems will re-surface; they will further divide attention, human resources and funds. The subject of Chapter 5, digital techniques comprise new problems brought by the pandemic from which global solutions might also eventually emerge. The broad questions there tackled – and not entirely answered – may apply to other emerging issues, old or new, as well. They can be summarised in a set of interrogations[1]:

> How far will the impact of a heavily digital-dependent way of life be? how many of the several newer usages will remain and replace old habits and procedures? what structural changes this may imply to society and the economy in the domestic realm, and to international competition and co-operation?

A full understanding of the replies to the above puzzle seems an impossible mission at this date. Independently of how deep and encompassing will be the answers, the unbridled higher penetration and percolation of the digital will make the need for new regulations clearer than before. Hopefully global, and dealing with the several aspects of "digital life", they are to be devised in a world where there will be neither much time nor a co-operative mood for the required negotiations. It may be guessed that societies will move closer to what has been experienced in China.

Security, combined with questions about individual liberties, will come to the fore. Coupled to the exponentially increasing communities' dependence on energy supplies and technological expertise, they raise a debate where the prevailing or desired forms of government must be seriously addressed. Given the bias evidenced during the pandemic, of states ever more resorting to digital controls, the "Chinese trend", despite with several nuances, risks becoming universal in the world corona changed.

Whatever the predicament, the amount of qualified human resources and technical knowledge required by the digital realm will contribute to widen the gap between advanced and technologically backward economies. An equivalent divide will be internal to the countries: digitally-inept citizens, comprising large fractions of the elderly, the illiterate, the poor and those who for some reason refuse to engage in a fully digital life, will be segregated from the digitally-wise citizens. A new dimension of inequality will prosper.

The more inward stance may lead to the improvement of domestic conditions, particularly as regards the day after of the pandemic. This may nurture globally inefficient or contradictory solutions, and a waste of precious funds, energy and time, if systematically overlooking the international dimension. In issues like many in the digital galaxy, politics, technology and strategy will become enmeshed, creating, if joint efforts and an open-minded attitude towards other countries' good practices are disregarded, confusion and pointless disputes.

Countries, once again in the frontline of the international scene, will be searching for more productive and pragmatic alliances. How out of focus their decisions will be depends on how they will value, in the difficult times ahead, longer term co-operative endeavours and a more careful redesign of the old order.

The climate change narrative will surely come back, as acknowledged in Chapter 1. As mentioned there, it is fair to wonder whether it will produce the desired fruits, in a far from peaceful and affluent post-Covid context, with political regimes and societies trying desperately to prove themselves they will survive minimally scathed.

An environmentally favourable China – though highly dependent on its economic health and the evolution of other alliances it may be involved in – will confront a still politically fractured US in this issue. With co-operation a scarcer good, already in huge demand be it for joint humanitarian actions, or in the debates on the international organisations' architecture, or on the digital realm and the fate of the information processing giants, less room will be left to the climate narrative. Greater enforcement, reduction targets and deeper rule-making will have to compete with all the previously mentioned dilemmas, as well as with the rearrangement, pushed by strategic considerations of the advanced economies, of the world's GVCs.

Nevertheless, two strands of the narrative may gain a certain momentum. One, favoured by influential groups in finance and business, will try to use it as a guiding excuse, or a true motivation for manifold developments and ventures, associated with a spectrum ranging from zero-carbon transition measures to green instruments and novel architectures in the financial realm.

The other refers to a revival of pollution abatement, whose benefits or consequences became clear and viral during the lockdowns, Tollefson (2020). This may find more acceptance and raise significant support for well-targeted policies; coupled with business opportunities, some progress may take place. Moreover, as in the golden times of the early environmental movement, Nixon (1972), when governmental support was instrumental for the creation of new (and later) powerful associations – Friends of the Earth, Greenpeace, among others – transforming outcomes are possible.

Air quality measures, matched with wiser control of transportation and displacement possibilities, better plastic and recycling handling policies, improved water quality and supply systems are some of the areas that could find nearly generalised goodwill, aided by their more or less direct impact on communities' health, and their role as a second-best help to poorer and harder hit countries. Infrastructure works and basic renewables' systems and devices may add volume and activities, in terms of jobs and demand. Tying their funding and support to the discussion on better health systems would indeed be a plus, making for an attractive win-win situation.

To the ambitious targets set forward by the EU and China, to become fossil fuels free by 2050 and 2060, respectively, a "greener US" may join in, setting also 2050, for instance, as a likely horizon.

There is no guarantee at all that these objectives will be fulfilled, but they will play a dual role in the coming years. One, of a sort of moral nature, furnishing an ideal or illusion to give more than a silver lining to the efforts to create a truly climate conscious normal. A second one, of a concrete character, to couch the ventures above into an apparently coherent effort, whose main outcome is to provide means for several activities and projects, minimising recession.

How much priority will be attached to them and how effective they will ultimately result are open questions.

6.3 Building blocks redux

A dynamic sketch of the world corona changed can evolve according to different hypotheses and viewpoints. At this point of the analysis, a few elements stand up as main pieces that will interact in any outlined macro-scenario. Like mathematical invariants, they will be present in any coming reality, and, together with the two defining axes adopted in this book, their varying intensity and combination will set the final scenario.

The state is definitely back, and this poses a curious indeterminacy to many analyses. It is back, in conflict with its own identity. It would be transforming, even revolutionary, if its new presumed autonomy could be effectively used to tackle and even solve a few of the main problems that will be common to all. A dangerous turn would be if its renewed importance translates into higher walls blocking foreign influences and exchanges.

Climate change is a good example. The standard rhetoric easily slips into the search for global solutions, requiring international agreements and institutions; but if the "global" is undeniably fundamental for many instances of the problem, there are others which will benefit when dealt bottom-up, with the state being the basic cell from where to generalise measures and behaviour. Signals up to now, and those recently from the US follow the same line, put forward encompassing costly schemes requiring substantial amounts of global funds. No mention is made on changing consumption patterns and the required national strategies for this, or on changing track from a blind economic growth assumption.

Instead of enforcing their own views of sustainability, usually backed by sophisticated financial and technological designs, relevant powers and groups should be confronted to other approaches, grounded on communities and large cities' decision-making. The pull from the global will probably dominate the discussions, but this alternative is not out of question yet. Middle power states are well positioned to seriously set game-changing examples.

Together with climate, inequality – with basic health and digital inequality included – and the digital galaxy are the three major dysfunctions that will demand attention; what by no means implies that reconstruction, in the broadest possible sense and with a zero-Covid goal, will not be forefront. How recovery efforts will combine with those for the three major issues is the key to ensure better or gloomier times.

Recovery, bluntly thought as back to the old normal, will tend to overtake them. In this event, all three will add to increased social tension, domestically controlled by the digital, internationally spread by similar digital techniques.

Problems will be tackled in a domestic and global dimension. Confusion and reverse inefficiencies, as pointed out before, risk making the domestic sometimes suboptimal and in conflict to other national solutions, but global risks may also jeopardise simpler and fairer solutions.

Geopolitics will live through this relative mess, as sketched in Chapter 4, and the greater the void in global governance the more weapons, nukes included, will be procured. The recent UK "defence budget upgrade" is more than symbolic. Perhaps, since the end of WWII, peace has never been more crucial and precious than in the coming years.

These elements allow the formulation of different macro-scenarios. But macro perspectives either hinder or gloss over several crucial questions that must be addressed. The remaining of this chapter presents a possible way to go deeper on such questions.

6.4 Selected scenarios

Following the framework exposed in Chapter 1, combination of the two axes there discussed, allowing two levels of intensity for each (from "lower/worse" to "too much/improved"), with the pre-coronavirus status at the "origin", gives way to a continuum of outcomes that may be synthesised into four background contexts, related to the possible quadrants.

The extreme ones, in terms either of less co-operation and worse relations, or improved co-operation *and* US-China relations, basically enhance or attenuate the problems previously discussed. The asymmetric ones – some to significant increases in co-operation coupled with a worsening of the US-Chinese relations, and the opposite combination – may provide more nuanced outcomes. The main feature in both pairs is that Chinese relevance as a world protagonist will increase; much in the former combination, more challenged by, and sometimes shared with the US, willingly or not, in the latter. The US, as the incumbent hegemon, has a more nuanced performance.

A third qualification, the degree and geographic scope of the recession, supposed also at two levels, in its worst version would diminish the role of the two main actors and, perhaps ironically, change to the better the co-operation stance of the other nations.

In overall terms, and assuming that no new and bold leadership will emerge in the near future, a more segregate world will come up, lost in several conflicts and conundrums, some already outlined. Immediate victims will be the weak and incapable international system and, as usual, the poorer nations. The extension of the fractures will be conditioned on how many key international issues could find a first and fast, if approximate, solution.

The analysis of any given specific issue benefits if departing from a chosen quadrant in the "co-operation x US-China" space. Three examples are discussed.

The fate of GVCs and globalisation of production in general

Globalisation has not ended with the pandemic, but its ways and lines of force are changing, requiring more diplomacy and careful planning to survive in the new environment. The temporary brake on the unrestricted flow of goods, services and people will linger on for some time; what about the retrenching of value chains and the widespread convergence of industry-related services?

Answers, either general or related to specific groups of sectors, will depend on which quadrant of the "co-operation x US-China" space the scenario will evolve.

Beginning with the worsening of relations, despite some improvement or back to normality in co-operation, it is expected that the Tech War together with economic relations as well will deteriorate, forcing the creation of two world-production nexuses, one to the West, centred in the US, and an Eastern one around China. The degree of decoupling will depend on how strong global co-operation will be, but value chains will predominantly be circumscribed to one of the regions, and geographically neighbouring economies will progressively enter into the nearer orbit. This does not necessarily mean reshoring of the chain, rather, many times, doubling it by also resorting to suppliers in the same side.

Middle powers, even when capable of standing as local hubs, will not be able to countervail this basic trend, as they lack the innovation capacity, funds and control over a wide technological spectrum that would allow for an extra, encompassing and more autonomous polarity. Countries like Japan, South Korea or Thailand, from one side, and Chile, Venezuela or Brazil, from the other, will be progressively compelled to redirect many economic flows to their regional focus. This will raise existential questions for those like Australia and New Zealand, a sort of Western bastions in the China Sea, or India and Russia, which would ideally prefer to keep an independent stance – more geared towards China, perhaps, as regards Russia – that is unlikely to survive.

Staying in the original quadrant, in perhaps a short time, separation may turn into divergence, encompassing norms and standards, and the design and re-organisation of quite a number of chains. Already existing niches, like the production mesh involving ASEAN, Japan, South Korea and China, will become denser; but they also generate substantial flows to the exterior, that will obligingly decrease.

The problem of cross-border chains and trade flows is neither simple nor evident. At the side of the niches, Germany, a Western economy, keeps significant interchanges, not necessarily linked to value chains, with China; flows hard to be entirely cut.

Most dramatically, about a quarter of intermediate goods used in high-tech exports from Japan, Korea, together with Mexico and the US, come from China nowadays. In sectors like the digital, telecoms, chemicals and pharma, US firms and key suppliers established in China have until now manifested a modest desire to relocate themselves. A few do want to return to their origins, some prefer to move to a nearby ASEAN economy, but a large majority in important sectors wants to keep their positions in China.

If co-operation further improves, this may be easier to accommodate: part of the established interconnections is able to subsist, though in a lower scale, and others may be spread among "friendly" or more neutral middle powers. Countries that are a final destination may continue to feel comfortable with the original structure, despite increasing the robustness of the chain by finding alternative suppliers in their side of the split. This is especially true for chains not directly related to crucial sectors, as some areas of pharma and medical equipment became. Ironically, for crucial sectors, as the final objective is availability and not relocations, multiplication may be tolerated, if a minimum of co-operation holds, or even stimulated, if it improves.[2]

Commodities flows may also find it easier to proceed in a close to normal pace; even cross-regional trade agreements, perhaps reduced in scope, may be kept or fixed.

The uneven recovery, if not adversely turning to China, will contribute to a brighter Eastern focus, increasing the distance between the bolder East and the West.

Moving to the fully negative quadrant, with less co-operation and worse relations, the divide will harden, with interactions less frequent and feasible: full decoupling may take place. Ideas like an alliance of "techno-democracies", apparently cherished by the new US administration, will go further in order to ultimately sever all technical exchanges with the Chinese realm. "Wrong-placed" or "independence-prone" countries, like Australia, Russia and India, will face uncomfortable decisions in terms of alliances.

The weaker Chinese position in services, where it is a net US importer, with some specific dependencies, may provoke further splits and changes in the value chains. A no-win situation can easily become real, what may act as an incentive for attempts to roll back.

In the case of better US-China relations, or ones in which at least the main problems are placed under controlled exchanges, without disturbing a mostly positive dialogue, many of the interrelated patterns and the associated value chains may be preserved. It is hard to think, in a more open relationship, despite with a persistent Tech War, that the superpowers will refuse to engage in diversified business integration ventures. A denser network of chains may help to avoid relations getting back to lower levels. The big tech firms, which already in the initial context could be a moderate force against the production divide, would move reasonably unfettered trying to deeper probe their competitive skills in the larger market.

The side and potentially important regions of the Middle East and Africa, neither source nor destination, apart from finished goods and commodities, of value chains, will follow whatever their attractors will do, playing a secondary role.

The Middle East, struggling to proceed at greater speed with the global energy transformation process, and lacking technological edge, will remain at the mercy of the two nexuses. Israel, the exception in terms of technology, may, like Russia, try to be as independent as possible. It is likely to continue so, as long as China does not show much interest in the region. Africa is doomed to stay – in any of the four background contexts – a field of fierce dispute by the two superpowers, something however irrelevant as regards the fate of GVCs in the short to mid run.

Global regulations for the main aspects of the digital world

The desire for harmonious international rules for the digital complex, heightened by the increase and higher penetration of digitisation in all aspects of life, also includes data privacy and security issues, topics intertwined with the chosen form of governance and political system. This example discusses the feasibility of achieving "the harmony" above mentioned, not specific aspects of the rules.

Though a consensus is starting to exist that the legal ways to deal with competitiveness, fair play and the freedoms associated with the digital must be, perhaps radically, different from those applied in standard economic sectors – something eventually realised, at great cost, in the case of the financial sector,[3] innovative approaches and methodological issues are still under strong debate. Benkler (2006) is one of the groundworks on this subject, not to be pursued here.

Again, it may be enlightening to start with the upper left quadrant: a worsening of relations, despite some improvement or back-to-normality in co-operation. As the Tech War and general economic relations become tougher, a first pattern of separation into two digital realms – similar to the case with GVCs – seems certain. To the separation of standards, devices and communication protocols, there will now be differentiation of rules and broad regulations and constraints. Nevertheless, three points make this divide different from the previous one.

The first is that the big techs in this case are extremely powerful, voracious and vocal: they will strive, as far as possible, to safeguard easy access to a world market.

The second is that increased rivalry and economic distancing does not imply the end of cross-communications. All countries will try to preserve the ability to reach, via diverse tele-modes, every other nation in the world; different regulations significantly impairing this may backfire against their own proposers. A minimal compatibility will always be requested and desired.

The third is that other countries, beyond the US and China, may have a voice in this case. They are either middle powers and small nations, like Russia, India, Israel, Estonia and even North Korea, with enough technical expertise to secure them an independent or influential role, or quite many others that, during the pandemic, moved further in exerting greater social control through digitisation and do not want to revert to the pre-Covid status. They wish to perfection and enlarge this facility, in their own terms, and will fight for a compromise between a minimum of global compatibility and a maximum of autonomy.

The two first points act against a complete independence of the regulations, at least a basic core having to be universally shared. Moreover, even if more than one of the previous international organisations may co-exist, as two or three ICANNs – the Internet Corporation for Assigned Names and Numbers, based in the US – or more than one other internet regulator, they are likely to be able to speak to each other, or warrant not too complex translations.

The third point operates in the opposite direction and individual, country-based decisions, and legislations may surge, creating a manifold of security, privacy and control information gathering and use norms. If the smart cities movement, heavily backed by the digital, progresses after the pandemic, confusion may come to lower governance levels, with the city many times being the basic legislative locus.

It seems unlikely that the two superpowers will succeed in imposing a wider uniformity in all these areas. The natural way to avoid a Babel-like context will be that a few homogenised approaches will prevail regionally, with country, and even city nuances covering minor issues.

The situation becomes more complex because of the interaction between norms and devices, mentioned in Chapter 5. Under the present scenario (quadrant), devices are likely to diverge along the two huge production nexuses.

The overall result will be a more fragmented world in terms of regulations and norms, with ultimately greater costs for individuals and firms, depending on their international exposure, and more idiosyncratic state controls, particularly though not necessarily only on the citizen. It will also translate into less compatibility and uniformity between all kinds of goods, making them, many times, more attractive.

The tech giants will hardly be able to achieve global supremacy but will certainly possess substantial market shares, while racing to reduce the size of their respective oligopolies. They may, depending on how intense co-operation will be, fix alliances across the main divide, with the common purpose of mutually increasing market penetration. However, their decision autonomy – as regards, for instance, the ability to freely dispose of individual accounts in social platforms, or decide about content – will be curbed.

Education and solid background expertise in the digital complex will become even more demanded, increasing inequalities and dependencies but allowing that, beyond the superpowers, countries like Russia, India and a few others regionally qualify as Masters of Algorithms – to use the expression in Chapter 5. Deeper technical knowledge will also be required for regulators, lawyers and policy makers dealing with the area, what again may give the already better-positioned countries an additional edge in the debates and chosen solutions, and channel technical exchanges, in semi-academic terms, between the two realms.

Conflict between states and platforms heightens when moving from this scenario to the downside right quadrant one. Improvement in US-China relations, nearly independently of the degree in international co-operation, will be a factor for more convergence; the desire to endorse geographically encompassing regulations increasing with the degree of co-operation, though ultimately limited by country-based preferences. Could a US-China understanding to restrict the power of the main platforms be envisaged?

84 *Dynamic sketches, detailed analyses*

In all scenarios, regional or other pre-existing associations, like the BRICS or the EU, may count in the final decisions. The latter enjoys one of the best accumulated experiences in all aspects of this vast area of regulation, being able to pursue its own objectives. As it does not host any of the big platforms, it is doubly entitled to play a very relevant, if not leading role. It is a sure power niche for the EU, provided it is not reluctant to assume a bolder position.

Adding the patchy recovery dimension, countries experiencing earlier improvements, if hosts of some expertise in the area, will be better able to impose or keep their options, in either side of the possible divide. However, the fast pace of developments, and the multiplicity of uses and applications that continually pop up, may easily turn their advantages – if not financially sustained – obsolete, weakening their voice in the debates.

Inequality prospects

A few qualifications are necessary before discussing the prospects of inequality within the rearrangements of power in the new reality.

Milanovic (2005) identifies three concepts when discussing world inequality. The first, when nations are taken as single units and the distribution of per capita income is studied. In the second, per capita incomes are weighed by population (in relative terms), and the resulting distribution is analysed. This is equivalent to endowing each individual in the world with his country's per capita income and then evaluating such distribution of people's income. In the third concept, the previous procedure is refined and individuals, inside each country, are endowed with the domestic income distribution. In all concepts, especially in the first two, outliers play a seriously distorting role. The main ones, due to the size of their population, are China and India, but very small countries, such as Brunei, Singapore, Qatar or Luxembourg, may also have a distorting effect.

The following discussion, though not focussed on precise quantitative distributional changes, assumes that whenever inequality among countries is mentioned, outliers are out. Moreover, inequality within each country is the main though not sole concern. Other dimensions of inequality are also investigated, as the digital divide or the access to basic health services, making sometimes the sheer income dimension only part of the problem.

With this proviso, the first scenario is placed in the downwards left quadrant, when a worsening takes place in both axes. Preliminary evidence suggests that, compared to richer countries, the impact of the pandemic on poorer countries has been more in terms of poverty increase than in deaths, Decerf et al. (2020). Within a given country, factoring out the lethality of the virus at the top layers of the age pyramid, the poor have identically been more affected. In this case, it seems that lockdowns hit unequally economic agents, leading distress to many low-income segments.

Under these assumptions, the status quo in the negative quadrant announces bad prospects. Without co-operation, and with escalating disagreement between the two powers there will be no room for improving the lot of the poorer countries. Middle powers will also be unable to significantly help as they themselves will be occupied with the increased domestic inequality gap. Contrary to some optimists, the digital divide will play a perverse role in this case, further alienating specific social classes and countries.

As forecasted in other situations addressed in this book, China may be a kind of "helper of last resort" in certain cases, including select African countries and strategic locations in the Belt and Road Initiative. Of course, if the recovery is faster, everything can be less bad.

Moving to the lower right quadrant, with the relationship improved, there will be room for both the US and China to act in favour of the poorer nations. This is more a wish, as the present rhetoric of "building back better", a bit surprisingly, stresses the environmental and digital questions, a certain production autonomy, a portfolio of technological priorities but overlooks the pressing poverty issue. Despite it may have been at the root of much suffering caused by the pandemic, Stiglitz (2020), poverty reduction is absent from most official statements on the reconstruction. The several packages delivered by the US and many middle powers are clearly insufficient for transforming the poverty-related, post-Covid status quo.

A more likely scenario in this quadrant is that middle powers will be better able to cope with their own inequalities as well as, to some extent, provide aid to less favoured neighbours or members of local alliances. This may be relatively effective in the case of Africa and Latin America. As trade is supposed to be less restricted in this scenario, indirect economic relief can come through this channel.

The positive behaviour becomes more consistent in the upper right quadrant, when the best combination of the two axes takes place. Nevertheless, this seems to be a more unrealistic scenario than the former, as co-operation – especially as regards inequality reduction – will be perhaps the most difficult thing to be achieved in the near future.

As in the famous sleepwalkers' metaphor, describing the unfortunate behaviour of nations and empires before WWI, the world corona changed, by failing to attend to the ever-present disfunction created by poverty and inequality, may be adding it to the stock of future global catastrophes.

Notes

1 The questions apply to any feature that became prominent during the pandemic; it suffices to replace the specific issue for the digital-related wording ("digital dependent way of life", "digital life", etc.).
2 An indirect example of this has been given since 2020 by China and Russia, enabling the final production of their respective vaccines in third countries, largely irrespective of their foreign policy affiliations. Western press has been quick to call it "vaccine diplomacy"; independently of their final strategic goals, both countries have set an example of the behaviour described in the text as possible and desirable.
3 A point cogently discussed in a nowadays famous 2009 article ("The quiet coup") by Simon Johnson, in the May issue of The Atlantic.

7 Conclusion

7.1 A not very optimistic reality

During crises, and the pandemic was no exception, it is common to hear pledges, calls, poems and wishful messages recited by groups or known personalities, that the day after will bring better attitudes, greater awareness of the other in general, and a more humanitarian, peaceful and constructive planet.

Positive hopes, the Bard could have said, are the essence of our dreams and an important help in any recovery or reconstruction endeavour. But from the starry night dream to the daylight problems and the remains left by the crisis, a long gap exists.

The sars.cov.2 virus and its variants, for reasons not quite clear yet, attacked mostly the developed Western nations and their near neighbours, like South America. Asia and Africa have been broadly more robust to it, but global connectivity has ensured widespread damage.

The world corona changed will be one of increasing multidimensional inequalities, with additional and diversified contingents of poor and no foreseeable solutions for related disfunctions, such as the refugees' issue or the educational and digital divide. Floating unemployment will be a permanent menace in the Western economies, while automation – with an extra help from the crisis – will pursue its encompassing invasion into diverse manufacturing and service sectors.

The digital will become more pervasive, enhancing patterns of dependence/inequality among nations – the masters of algorithms dominating "the rest" – and within societies – digital illiteracy becoming a sort of social disease to the poor, the old and the less educated. The needed global regulation for this Kraken fully awakened by the pandemic will most likely not be global, remaining at best regional and expectedly piecemeal, geographically and thematically, though some basic harmony may be preserved at high and unstable costs.

88 Conclusion

The huge nebula of cybersecurity, carrying fake news, invasion of privacy, unfair and unsuspected modes of competition and control, will be one of the great victims of the lack of encompassing co-ordination on the digital. The key super-structure enabling modern societies will be vulnerable.

Already a consequence more than a trend will be the decrease in individual and citizenship power; the after-corona members of the back-to-relevant nation states will be highly controlled and more defenceless citizens. Multiple surveillance mechanisms are due to provoke ever-growing social and political tensions, as less personal freedom will match more dissatisfaction and questioning of the public structure and institutions.

The revered transformative promise of the digital, despite positive empowerment of certain less favoured groups, will tend to the negative and frustrating. The authoritarian features it easily engenders will raise new political and cultural concerns.

Having held an isolated stance during the pandemic, accompanied by an aggressive if not military rhetoric among them and towards players in the world health sector, less prone to co-operation and experiencing doubtful sympathy, nations – involved in a vicious cycle of predatory behaviour – will systematically strive under the threat of the obligation to return to some normalcy.

They will be mostly judged as Efficient or Non-efficient Leviathans, with other important dimensions unfortunately overlooked. Auspicious windows of opportunity opened by the renewed concern and importance of the state are likely to be lost. The urge "to clear up the mess" and "to provide relief after relief" will leave no time to rethink state power under a more modern framework, in which it would be a partner in the struggle for social improvement and not merely the other side of a private-public divide.

Despite high hopes and speeches, and frequent fake or biased-information media campaigns for humanitarian values and sustainability, the profiteering and success logic will dominate the coming moments.

In such a world, it is almost unavoidable that the US-China relationship slowly and steadily moves to a split between the two. How deep this will run depends on multiple factors and, also, chance events. Widespread military confrontation seems unwanted, but local attritions, aggressive finger-pointing and harsh economic disputes will break out. In a world heavily armed and with a proliferation of nukes, the security passport in a less co-operative and starker rivalry context, disasters may happen.

The split will bring novel features, be they in the interaction between telecom systems, protocols and related devices, or, in a larger spectrum, in the invisible agents and facilitators of global reach, from bar codes to accounting practices, industrial norms and standards. Higher costs and moderate chaos may ensue. The cleavage can also be reinforced by the progressive transformation of financial markets, thanks to the introduction of digital money, the continuation of their eastwards-move and additional uncertainties derived from the recession with fiscal fragility.

Independently of becoming more or less clearly bipolar, the world will be also mildly polycentric. Regional exchanges will become denser and constellations of middle powers – never holding the quasi-absolute power of the two giants – may enjoy for a variety of reasons, restricted though significant policy spaces. Specific technological know-how or natural endowments, and strategic geographic positions combined with respectable military capabilities are a few main ones. In such a set-up, Africa, for instance, may find interesting opportunities, while Asia will steadily tread to ever more autonomy.

It is in this global scenario, detailed in some of its key aspects in the preceding chapters, that a recovery will take place: a recovery, not a step towards a world more concerned with distributional and global pressing issues. In fact, the major open question is: a recovery to what and to where?

7.2 Is there another side?

Progress and its associated economic concept, growth, are well-known as elusive and hard to grasp ideas. The more one gets into details and seeks to understand its myriad mechanisms and why they are usually considered beneficial, the more riddles and unveiled interactions appear, and renewed doubts surface. Like democracy, maybe they are debatable goals used or rather pursued for lack of better alternatives.

Will the reality when the pandemic comes under control be a cradle for progress? It is hard to answer, given the numerous problems, new and old, that will be requiring attention; a reliable evaluation is too demanding, an ultimately scalar measure almost impossible to conceive. Several conflicting forces will be in action.

Take cities, for instance. On one side, centrifugal strains will be pushing for less agglomeration and lower density: the perhaps 20 per cent of the labour force who will remain in home office; the attraction of an easier control of social distancing and a better positioning for the remaining and (probably) coming contagion issues; improved management of public systems in a smaller conurbation, and also of energy supply risks – thanks to the greater facility in designing back-up systems; and savings in transportation with corresponding less polluted surroundings.

On the other side, centripetal energies that make large cities a unique centre of innovation and job creation will not vanish. Scale effects translate also into higher quality and diversification in all kinds of services: more specialised hospitals; better schools; better and multiple opportunities for young professionals; increased, denser and more enlightened social and cultural life. A strong and vibrant metropolis will be a valuable barrier against the unavoidable centralizing trend of central, or federal, governments.

The outcome in each particular case can vary, depending on which combination of these effects will prevail. Drawing on a telling image by urban specialist Richard Florida, the US without New York, San Francisco and Chicago is not the US, or in the same token, France without Paris, Marseille and Lyon, or Brazil without São Paulo and Rio de Janeiro. Most metropolises will adapt and thrive; many smaller ones will also thrive and survive; others will drastically change or vanish.

The new normal will be different from the one in 2018. How much, is again difficult to gauge, as a complex, shifting globality is in motion. With a bit of tolerance, one may admit that a few main reasons why have been expounded in this text. The final point to be taken into consideration is that the "different" will also be transitional: the world after cov.vars.2 will not be static, *it will continue to change.*

The framework here outlined delineates this next moment, probably a less optimistic and more egoistic one, but contrary to hurried interpretations of the Hegelian historical stages, just a moment, not an end. A less optimistic scenario is not necessarily a pessimistic one. It will be an instant prone to further developments and new rearrangements that, once the tensions and conflicts it contains are diffused or, more analytically, equated, may bring greater co-operation and concern to the cause of the planet and our humanity. Or not.

Bibliography

Ackerman, E. and J. Stavridis. 2021. *2034: A Novel of the Next World War*. New York: Penguin Press.
Allison, G. 2017. *Destined for War: Can America and China Escape Thucydides Trap?* Boston, MA: Houghton Mifflin Harcourt.
Beck, U. 2016. *The Metamorphosis of the World*. Cambridge: Polity Press.
Benkler, Y. 2006. *The Wealth of Networks*. New Haven, CT and London: Yale University Press.
Bostrom, N. 2014. *Superintelligence: Paths, Dangers, Strategies*. Oxford: Oxford University Press.
Chuanying, L. 2020. Forging stability in cyberspace. *Survival* 62(2), April–May; 125–35.
Crouch, C. 2004. *Post-Democracy*. Cambridge: Polity Press.
Decerf, B., F. H. G. Ferreira, D. G. Mahler and O. Sterck. 2020. *Lives and Livelihoods: Estimates of the Global Mortality and Poverty Estimates of the COVID-19 Pandemic*. World Bank Policy Research Working Paper 9277, June. Washington, DC: The World Bank.
Flôres, R. G., Jr. 2020. Back to nukes? Global Governance's transitional moment, in L. Grigoryev and A. Pabst, eds., *Global Governance in Transformation: Challenges for International Co-operation*. Cham: Springer Nature Switzerland.
Friedland, W. H., L. Busch, F. H. Buttel and A. P. Rudy, eds. 1991. *Towards a New Political Economy of Agriculture*. Boulder, CO: Westview Press.
Hopkins, R. F. and D. J. Puchala. 1978. Perspectives on the international relations of food. *International Organization* 32(3) (Special Issue: The Global Political Economy of Food); 581–616.
Howard, M. 1976. Order and conflict at sea in the 1980s. Adelphi Paper 124, reprinted as Chapter Fifteen in IISS, 2020, *A Historical Sensibility: Sir Michael Howard and The International Institute of Strategic Studies, 1958–2019*. London: Routledge.
Ikenberry, J. 2020. The next liberal order. *Foreign Affairs* 99(4), July–August; 133–42.

Bibliography

Mahbubani, K. 2008. *The New Asian Hemisphere: The Irresistible Shift of Global Power to the East.* New York: PublicAffairs.

Mazzucato, M. 2018. *The Value of Everything: Making and Taking in the Modern Economy.* New York: PublicAffairs.

McPhail, T. L. 1987. *Electronic Colonialism: The Future of International Broadcasting and Communication.* Newbury Park, CA: SAGE Publications.

Milanovic, B. 2005. *Worlds Apart: Measuring International and Global Inequality.* Princeton, NJ: Princeton University Press.

Mouritzen, H. 2017. Small states and Finlandisation in the Age of Trump. *Survival* 59(2), April–May; 67–84.

Münchau, W. 2021. Our worst policy error. EVRO Intelligence, 23 January 2021; available at //eurointelligence.com/column/vaccines.

Nixon, R. M. 1972. Environmental quality, in D. L. Thompson, ed., *Politics, Policy and Natural Resources.* New York: Free Press.

Nye, J. 2011. Nuclear lessons for cyber security? *Strategic Studies Quarterly* 5(4); 18–38.

Rosenau, J. 2004. Strong demand, huge supply: governance in an emerging epoch, in I. Bache and M. Flinders, eds., *Multi-level Governance.* New York: Oxford University Press.

Russell, B. 1945. *The History of Western Philosophy* (1972 copyright edition). New York: Simon & Schuster, Inc.

Scheidel, W. 2017. *The Great Leveler: Violence and the History of Inequality from the Stone-Age to the Twentieth Century.* Princeton, NJ: Princeton University Press.

Sen, A. 1981. *Poverty and Famines: An Essay on Entitlement and Deprivation.* Oxford: Clarendon Press.

Stiglitz, J. 2020. Conquering the great divide. *Finance and Development* 57(3), September; 17–9.

Tegmark, M. 2018. *Life 3.0.* UK: Penguin Books, Penguin Random House.

Tharoor, S. and S. Saran. 2020. *The New World Disorder and the Indian Imperative.* New Delhi: Aleph Book Company.

Tollefson, J. 2020. How the coronavirus pandemic slashed carbon emissions – in five graphs. *Nature* 582(7811), June; 158–9.

Valladão, A. G. A. 2014. Masters of the algorithms: the geopolitics of the new digital economy from Ford to Google. Discussion Paper, *German Marshall Fund of the United States and OCP Policy Centre.* Brussels: German Marshall Fund Office.

Wallerstein, I., R. Collins, M. Mann, G. Derluguian and C. Calhoun. 2013. *Does Capitalism have a Future?* Oxford: Oxford University Press.

World Bank. 2020. *Reversal of Fortune: Poverty and Shared Prosperity Report.* Washington, DC: The World Bank.

Index

Ackerman, E. 20
administration: Biden 38; Obama II 44; second Obama 14; second of President Clinton 63; Trump 16
Afghanistan 14
Africa 14, 15, 20, 25, 41, 49, 55–7, 72, 81, 85, 87, 89
Ali-Baba 61
alliances 2, 6, 33, 43, 44, 48, 54, 55, 71, 73, 75, 81, 83; country 67; credible 22; durable 38; effective 45; forged 38; hunting for 21; local 85; pragmatic 75; regional 56; shifting 9, 53; traditional 18; unstable 22
Allison, G. 13, 20
Alphabet 61
Amazon 61
America(s) 16, 57; Central 20, 54; Central and South 15, 56; Latin 85; South 14, 20, 45, 54, 87; South and Central 54; South and Latin 48
Andean Community 57
Apple 61
Argentina 46, 48, 57
artificial intelligence 19, 62, 65, 67
Asia 8, 14, 15, 20, 39, 40, 42, 54, 55, 72, 87, 89; East 15; Southeast 39, 41
Asian Infrastructure and Development Bank (AIIB) 15
Association of South-East Asia Nations -ASEAN 15, 20, 38–40, 43, 47, 49, 54, 80
Australia 37, 39, 54, 79, 81

Baidu 61
Bangladesh 61
Beck, U. 25
Belgium 52
Belt and Road Initiative (BRI) 15, 85
Benkler, Y. 82
Berlin Wall 1, 13
Biden, J. R. 18, 19
bipolar 89
blockchain 65
Bolivia 57
Borrell, J. 50
Bostrom, N. 62
Brazil 2, 5, 34, 37, 41, 45, 46, 57, 62, 65, 68, 73, 79, 90
Bretton Woods: constructs 32; institutions 23, 31; order 23; system 12, 34; times 24
BRICS 30, 37, 41, 48, 49, 84; New Development Bank 16
Brunei 84
Bush, G. W. 13

Canada 34, 48
Caribbean 21
Chad 57
Chile 79
China-US: pair 38
Chuanying, L. 67
climate 3, 4, 76, 77; change 45, 49, 75, 77; issue 16; narrative 76
Coalition for Epidemic Preparedness Innovations 25, 26
Cold War 20, 32, 34, 55

94　*Index*

companies: information technology 33; US 39
co-operation 3, 8, 9, 24, 37, 44, 74, 75, 78–80, 82, 83, 85, 88, 90; agreement 44; drive 56; international 83; stance 78; x US-China space 79; world 19
co-operative 73, 88; bonds 25; Covid-reality 73; dimension 51; endeavours 75; environment 68; mood 74; world 23, 55
corona(virus) 2–4, 8, 22, 25, 35, 40, 53, 58, 63; after- 43, 88; crisis 37; post- 6,8, 29, 30, 44–6, 57, 65–7, 75, 77, 85, 87; pre- 44, 74, 78
COVAX 25, 26
Covid(-19): 4, 23, 26, 44, 49, 72; crisis 35; post- 32, 42, 47, 75, 85; pre- 14, 18, 25, 30, 82; zero- 77; *see also* co-operative
Crouch, C. 61
Cuba 14
cybersecurity 66, 68
Czech Republic 50

data protection 65, 66
Decerf, B. 85
Delors, J. 50, 63
democracy(ies) 1, 6, 7, 24, 38, 51, 61, 73, 89; format of 31; illiberal 49; Indian 7; lack of 12; techno- 80; US 7
democratic 70; enterprises 7; deficit 50; institutions 40; nations 31; values 6, 7, 22
Deng Xiaoping 11
digital 5, 9, 29, 51, 59–65, 67, 68, 78, 80, 82, 83, 85, 87, 88; complex 4, 5, 9, 28, 59, 67, 71, 74, 75, 78, 81, 83; dependence 65; dependent 74; developments 69; divide 84, 85, 87; galaxy 4, 28, 49, 59, 62, 64, 66, 75, 77; inequality 77; life 74, 75; money 89; nebulae 67; platforms 61; realm(s) 64, 66, 75, 82; sphere 62; subsectors 14; techniques 74, 78; transactions 68, 69; viewpoint 70; yuan 68
digitally 13, 60, 63, 67; inept 75; wise 75

dual-circulation theory 15

Egypt 44, 52, 53
electronic colonialism 81
entitlement 63, 64
Estonia 82
Eurasia 15, 49
Eurogroup 51
Europe 52; Central 47, 49; Western 62
European Commission (EC) 50
European Intervention Initiative (EI2) 50
European Union (EU) 7, 16, 17, 26, 34, 37, 44–54, 62, 65, 66, 69, 76, 84

Facebook 61, 69
financial 16, 19, 48, 60, 70; architecture 51; clout 22, 42, 69; compensation 17; crisis(es) 29, 31; feasibility 51; incentive 66; instruments 51; markets 68, 89; realm 76; sector 82; and stock markets 27; system 5, 11, 19, 68; and tax schemes 4; and technological designs 77; transactions 37
Finland 55
Flôres, R. G., Jr 61
Florida, R. 90
Food and Agriculture Organisation (FAO) 5
foreign direct investment (FDI) 37, 39, 57
France 33, 47, 48, 50, 52. 90
Friedland, W. H. 63
Friends of the Earth 76

G7 30
G20 30
General Agreement on Tariffs and Trade (GATT) 31, 32
Georgia 47
Germany 47–50, 52, 64, 80
Global Alliance for Vaccines and Immunisation (GAVI) 25, 26
Google 61, 69
Greenpeace 76
group(s): Ant, Ant Ma 19, 61; focus 30; influential 76; interest 70; less favoured 88; of middle powers

44; opinion 21; of sectors 79; ultimately US- 54; Western 7
Gulf States 44

health 4, 24, 76; conditions 7; economic 75; and epidemic control 46; global 49; hazards 56; initiatives 56; instruments 34; order 25; public 4, 24–6; question 25; and risk management 27; sector 88; services 84; status 49; system(s) 38, 76
Hegel, G. W. F. 1, 2
Hegelian 3, 9, 90
Hong Kong 3, 15–17
Hopkins, R. F. 63
Howard, M. (Sir) 21
Huawei 17, 66
Hungary 47, 50, 73

Ikenberry, J. 31
India 2, 5, 32, 34, 37, 39, 40, 41, 43, 45, 48, 52, 54–7, 64, 72, 73, 79, 81–4
Indonesia 15, 34, 52, 55
inequality(ies) 5, 40, 57, 60, 75, 77, 84, 86; gap 85; health and digital 77; and health problems 40; multidimensional 87; reduction 60, 85; world 84; *see also* digital
institution(s) 3, 23, 25, 26, 28, 30, 31, 33–5, 57, 69, 77, 88; democratic 40; financial 30; hierarchical 32; international 3, 10, 24, 29, 34, 35, 66; multilateral 9, 16, 23, 67, 73; public health 34; regional 25, 34; research 51; *see also* Bretton Woods
International Health Regulations (IHR) 25–7, 34
International Monetary Fund (IMF) 30
International Telecommunications Union (ITU) 66
Internet Corporation for Assigned Names and Numbers (ICANN) 84
Iran 14. 43–5, 52–4, 66
Iranian régime 52
Iraq 14, 43, 44, 52
Islam 52, 52

Islamic 43, 49, 52, 53
Islamic State of Iraq and Syria (ISIS) 57
Israel 32, 81, 82

Japan 11, 15, 16, 20, 35, 39, 41–3, 47, 54. 56, 79, 80
Joint Comprehensive Plan of Action (JCPOA) 44

Kazakhstan 48
Kissinger, H. 50
Koran 52
Korea(s) 40, 42, 43, 47, 56; North 42, 66, 82; South 11, 39, 54, 56, 64, 79, 80

Lampedusa, T. di 28
Lebanon 43
Libya 45
lockdown(s) 5, 30, 38, 53, 60, 65, 72, 76, 85
Luxembourg 84

Ma, J. 19
Maghreb 57
Mahbubani, K. 8, 43
Malaysia 39
Mali 57
masters of algorithms 63, 69, 83, 87
Mazzucato, M. 63
McPhail, T. L. 61
Mercosul 46, 49, 57
Mexican standoff 43
Mexico 48, 57, 80
Microsoft 61
Middle East 14, 43, 44, 55, 57, 67, 72, 81
middle power(s) 3, 6, 9, 20–2, 29, 31, 36–9, 41, 43, 45–8, 51, 54, 62, 68, 71, 77, 79, 80, 82, 85, 89; *see also* group(s)
Milanovic, B. 84
military 20; aid 32; application(s) 15, 64, 67; capabilities 70, 89; confrontation 20, 88; rhetoric 88; and security dimension 43; technologies 19, 40; *see also* power
Mogherini, F. 50
Moldavia 47

Mouritzen, H. 55
Mozambique 57
multilateral 15, 19, 44; approach 30, 32, 74; credo 16; features 34; stance 33; *see also* organisation(s)
multilateralism 2, 30–4
multipolarity 22
Münchau, W. 51
Muslim 3, 7, 43, 52, 53

natural endowments 89
Nehru, J. 40, 55
Netherlands 66
New Zealand 39, 54, 79
Next Generation EU 51, 69
Niger 57
Nigeria 34, 48, 56. 57
Nixon, R. M. 72
norms: and regulations 17; and standards 80, 89
North Atlantic Treaty Organisation (NATO) 16, 34, 47, 48, 50
nuclear 45; armament 42, 46; disasters 35; power 41; proliferation 31
nukes 46, 78, 88
Nye, J. 66

Obama, B. 17
organisation(s) 2, 9, 24–7, 35, 59; global 27; international 3, 9, 15, 23, 31, 32, 34, 69, 75, 82; multilateral 31, 32; regional 48

Pakistan 41, 52, 54–6
Paris Agreement 4
Parmenides 3
People's Republic of China (PRC) 14, 16, 19
Persian Gulf 41, 43, 52
pharma 28, 80; big 26
Philippines 15
platform(s) 29, 63, 83; big 70, 84; diplomacy 69; owners 69; social 83
Poe, E. A. 6
Poland 47, 50, 73
polycentric 89
poverty 5, 44, 56, 85; absolute 12; dire 40; extreme 12; and inequality 86; multidimensional 5; reduction 85; related 85
power: arithmetic of 58; balance of 55; dispersion of 37; and example 38; military 43, 67; regional 34, 37, 42
protectionism 38
Puchala, D. J. 63
Putin, V. 47

Qatar 45, 53, 84

rare earths 19, 54
recession 5, 29, 56, 57, 68, 72, 73, 76, 78, 89
recovery(ies) 5, 9, 25, 35, 56, 57, 67, 69, 72, 77, 78, 80, 84, 84, 87, 89
Regional Comprehensive Economic Partnership (RCEP) 39–42, 56
regulations 15, 66, 74, 82–4; global 87; market 63; and norms 83; *see also* norms
Romania 50
Roosevelt, F. D. 24
Rosenau, J. 32
Russell, B. 3
Russia 6, 14, 32, 34, 40, 42, 44, 46–8, 54, 55, 57, 64, 66, 79–83; *see also* US-Russia

Saran, S. 63
Saudi Arabia 16, 44, 52–4
scenario(s) 3, 5, 7–9, 39, 44, 57, 65, 70, 72, 73, 77–9, 83–5, 89, 90
Scheidel, W. 72
security 16, 31, 65, 66, 75, 82; aspects 57; concerns 46; dimension 43; entities 67; issues 6, 54, 62, 65, 81; measures 66; passport 88; structure 39
Sen, A. 63
Serbia 48
Shi'a 43, 44, 52
Singapore 39, 84
Snowden, E. 65
Somalia 57
South Africa 48
South China Sea 3, 14–6, 21, 42
Southern Cone 46

Soviet Union (USSR) 37; dissolution of 13; post- 46 spheres of authority 32
Spinoza 3
standards 17, 49, 80, 82; *see also* norms; technological
Stavridis, J. 20
Stiglitz, J. 85
Sunni 43, 44
superpower(s) 9, 34, 37, 41
Syria 43, 45, 52

Taiwan 3, 15, 16; Strait 13–14
technological: challenge 17; competence 51; design 5, 77; edge(s) 64, 81; expertise 75; feature 9; and financial clout 42; innovation 63; inputs 66; know-how 89; links 5; priorities 85; prowess 42; spectrum 79; and standards dimensions 45
technologically-backward 75
technology 14, 15, 38, 41, 55, 65, 67, 70, 71, 75, 81; battery 65; Chinese, Chinese 5G 66; high- 17, 70; leadership 14; low- 11; transfer 17; transformational 70; *see also* companies
technology war (Tech War) 16, 18–20, 54, 65, 67, 70, 79, 81, 82
Tegmark, M. 62
Tencent 61
Thailand 15, 39, 79
Tharoor, S. 63
Tiannamen Square 11
Tollefson, J. 72
Treaty of Lisbon 50
Trump, D. 2, 13, 14, 16–18
Turkey 37, 43–5, 52, 54, 55, 57

Ukraine 47
United Arab Emirates (UAE) 52, 53
United Kingdom (UK) 33, 48, 60, 78

United Nations (UN) 5, 24, 33–5, 45, 74; agencies 34; Convention on the Law of the Seas 32; General Assembly 4; Security Council 33, 74; specialised agencies 15; Sustainable Development Goals 4; system 36; Universal Declaration of Human Rights 7; World Conference in Sendai 35; World Food Programme 5
Uruguay 46
Uruguay Round 28, 64
US-China 9; dialogue 44; opposition 53; relations 78, 81; relationship 8, 18, 20, 56, 67, 88; rivalry 52; understanding 83; *see also* co-operation
US-Russia: relations 3

vaccine(s) 24, 26, 27, 38, 41, 44, 46, 48, 50, 51, 53; Covid-19 25
Valladão, A. 63
value chain(s) 39, 68, 79–81; global (GVCs) 15, 28, 42, 63, 68, 76, 81, 82; exchanges 37
Venezuela 57, 79
Vietnam 15, 17

Wallerstein, I. 61
weapons 78; of mass destruction 6; nuclear 14, 37, 40; technology 46
Weber, M. 31
World Bank 5
World Health Assembly 26, 37
World Health Organisation (WHO) 17, 23–30, 34
World Trade Organisation (WTO) 13, 16, 23, 27–31

Xi Jinping 13, 15
Xinjiang 16

Yemen 52

Taylor & Francis eBooks

www.taylorfrancis.com

A single destination for eBooks from Taylor & Francis with increased functionality and an improved user experience to meet the needs of our customers.

90,000+ eBooks of award-winning academic content in Humanities, Social Science, Science, Technology, Engineering, and Medical written by a global network of editors and authors.

TAYLOR & FRANCIS EBOOKS OFFERS:

A streamlined experience for our library customers

A single point of discovery for all of our eBook content

Improved search and discovery of content at both book and chapter level

REQUEST A FREE TRIAL
support@taylorfrancis.com

For Product Safety Concerns and Information please contact our EU
representative GPSR@taylorandfrancis.com
Taylor & Francis Verlag GmbH, Kaufingerstraße 24, 80331 München, Germany

www.ingramcontent.com/pod-product-compliance
Lightning Source LLC
Chambersburg PA
CBHW051757230426
43670CB00012B/2328